PLAZA

BEST
*From the Interior
Design Magazine
Hall of Fame*

A Vitae Publication

Table of Contents

 Marvin B. Affrime, 14

 Davis Allen, 18

 Benjamin Baldwin, 22

 Donald Brinkmann, 36

 Thomas Britt, 40

 R. Scott Bromley, 44

 Mario Buatta, 48

 Orlando Diaz-Azcuy, 68

 Angelo Donghia, 72

 Henry End, 74

 Billy W. Francis, 78

Florence Knoll Bassett, 130
Sarah Tomerlin Lee, 134
Naomi Leff, 138
Neville Lewis, 142

Charles Pfister, 162
Warren Platner, 166
Donald D. Powell, 170
Robert D. Kleinschmidt, 170

Betty Sherrill, 190
Sally Sirkin Lewis, 194
Ethel Smith, 198
Andre Staffelbach, 202

Carleton Varney, 220
Lella Vignelli, 224
Massimo Vignelli, 224
Kenneth H. Walker, 228

Robert Metzger, 146

Juan Montoya, 150

Frank Nicholson, 154

Mrs. Henry Parish II, 158

William L. Pulgram, 174

Andrée Putman, 178

Rita St. Clair, 182

John F. Saladino, 186

Philippe Starck, 206

Stanley Tigerman, 212

Margaret McCurry, 212

Adam D. Tihany, 216

Tod Williams, 232

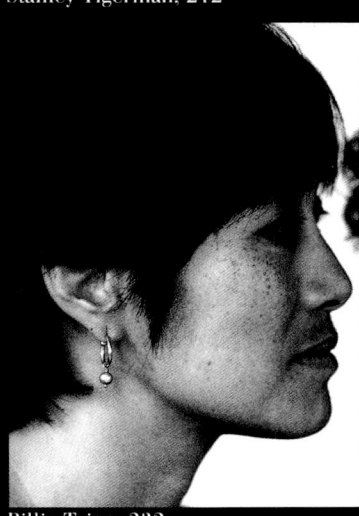
Billie Tsien, 232

BE

ST

*From the Interior
Design Magazine
Hall of Fame*

*Introduction by: Stanley Abercrombie
Text by: Pirrie B. Aves, Bret Parsons,
Nicholas Polites, Mary Jane Pool
Design by: Massimo Vignelli*

*A Vitae Publication
Vitae Publishing, Inc.,
Grand Rapids, Michigan*

Copyright 1992 Vitae Publishing, Inc.

All rights reserved under International and Pan-American copyright conventions. Published in the United States by Vitae Publishing, Inc.; 800 Grand Plaza Place; Grand Rapids, MI 49503

LIBRARY OF CONGRESS CATALOGING-IN-PUBLICATION DATA
BEST
From the Interior Design Hall of Fame
p.   cm.
Includes Index
ISBN 0-9624596-6-6
ISBN 0-9624596-8-2 (soft)
1. Interior decorators—United States—Biography. 2. Interior decoration—United States—History—20th century. I. Aves, John C., 1942-   . II Interior Design (New York, N.Y.)
NK2004.2.I58 1992
729'. 092'2—dc20
[B]
92-27941
CIP

VITAE PUBLISHING, INC.
Chairman: John C. Aves
President: James C. Markle

Editor: John C. Aves
Assistant Editor: Pirrie B. Aves
Contributing Editor: Bret Parsons
Contributing Editor: Nicholas Polites
Contributing Editor: Mary Jane Pool
Introduction: Stanley Abercrombie
Publishing Coordinator: Sheri Rambaud
Communications Coordinator: Cynthia A. Vandecar

AVES INC.
Art Coordinator: Carol Dungan
Production Artist: Nancy J. Allen
Production Supervisor: Douglas Koster
Financial Management: Robert Spaman

USA distributor to the trade:
Watson-Guptill Publications
1515 Broadway, New York, NY 10036
ISBN #0-8230-6248-1

International distributor:
Rockport Publishers, Inc.
146 Granite Street
Rockport, MA 01966
ISBN #962 4596-6-6

Printed in Singapore by Toppan
Typeset in USA by Vitae Publishing, Inc.

Cover Photos (left to right):
Thomas Britt, William Hodgins,
Charles Pfister and Michael Graves

Foreword

The most indelible footprints of our civilization are the buildings and interiors that we leave behind. These are the hieroglyphics of our age, the symbols that will tell future generations about our contributions. They carry the subtleties of style, and therefore the emotional tone of our age. The interiors in which we work, raise families, entertain and rest are the most personal journals of our time.

A book which attempts to present the best of all the hundreds of designers of this era requires an impartial third party selection. No one person has the omniscience to discern the finest homes of every region or the most important institutional projects. Therefore, the Interior Design Magazine Hall of Fame is a logical touchstone because it bridges all types of interior design and is not partial to any region, trend or professional organization.

The 76 architects and designers who have been nominated to the Interior Design Magazine Hall of Fame are the master artists who have expressed this important facet of our culture. Most have thriving design practices today and are at work shaping the way we will look at the turn of the millennium. This retrospective looks back at the most famous designers and architects of our age; it also looks ahead from the viewpoint of these visionary creative people.

BEST is dedicated in memory of my late father, Wesley Aves, on the occasion of the 50th Anniversary of the communications company he founded, which published this book.

John C. Aves

Introduction

It seems perfectly natural that the profession of interior design should maintain a Hall of Fame. It is a profession, after all, that has palpable, unmistakable stars, a profession that truly enjoys honoring them, a profession that likes any good excuse for a big, kissy, dress-up celebration.

So it may seem strange that the Interior Design Magazine Hall of Fame was instituted as recently as 1985. It began, as so many things do, as a response to a need, that of an organization called the Foundation for Interior Design Education Research (or, more familiarly, FIDER). Founded in 1971, FIDER is the body responsible for accrediting schools of interior design in the United States and Canada and thus plays a critical role in the field's progress towards greater professionalism. FIDER's work, however, is expensive.

This was the subject of a phone call early in 1985 from Frank Judson to Lester Dundes, the publisher of *Interior Design*. The year before, Judson had been honored upon his retirement as vice chairman of Stroheim & Romann, the prominent fabrics firm, and the event had been a successful fund-raiser for FIDER. Judson suggested another such benefit, this time honoring Dundes. It seemed a good idea: Dundes, 71 years old, but with the energy level of a teenager—outgoing, outspoken, sometimes outrageous—was a legendary and much admired character in the field. There was no one who didn't know Lester, almost no one who wouldn't buy a pricey ticket for the honor of toasting him. He told Judson he'd think about it. He called Judson back with an even better idea: the institution of a Hall of Fame at a ceremony that would become an annual event, *the* annual event, with FIDER the perennial beneficiary.

Plans were ambitious right from the start. The event would be held in the mammoth Grand Ballroom of the Waldorf-Astoria, a room recently restored in a grand manner by Kenneth Hurd. There would be dinner; there would be dancing; it would be *lots* of money per plate; it would be, of course, black tie; it would be, of course, a great success.

In June of 1985, a card was bound into the current issue of *Interior Design* asking subscribers to nominate "the best and most influential professionals now at work," a date of December 2nd was engaged at the Waldorf, and the lofty ambitions for the evening were entrusted to the magazine's development director, Janice Langrall, who found herself in a strange new world of tablecloths, table assignments, audio-visual presentations and more; there were decisions to be made about food, the orchestra, the color of candlesticks. Alberto Paolo Gavasci, the magazine's creative director, designed plaques to be given to the honorees, and Italian metalsmiths were put to work on them.

Meanwhile, reservations for seats and for entire tables began to pour in, as many as Lester had dreamed of, more than most of us had dared hope for; in the end, the ballroom was filled to overflowing and has been every year since.

Even more exciting, readers' votes for Hall of Fame members were coming in. That first year, as announced, final choices were made from the many nominees by *Interior Design*'s publisher and editors. We wanted a large group in order to firmly establish the Hall of Fame; as in the composition of our magazine's contents, we wanted a geographic diversity, we wanted both men and women, we wanted both residential and contract designers, we wanted a variety of stylistic expressions to be represented, and we wanted the very best. Hall of Fame fever was upon us as we debated the choices. We made lists, we debated, we made more lists, we voted. Finally, 16 designers were chosen as the Hall of Fame's charter members: Davis Allen, Benjamin Baldwin, Florence Knoll Bassett, Mario Buatta, Barbara D'Arcy, Angelo Donghia (who, tragically, died before the induction ceremony and was honored posthumously), Henry End, Arthur Gensler, Richard Himmel, Melanie Kahane, Lawrence Lerner, Mrs. Henry Parish II, Warren Platner, John Saladino, Michael Taylor and Ken Walker.

And there was one more decision. In order to emphasize that this would be an institution not for the narrow interests of our magazine, but for the entire profession, we gave a special award to the influential and powerful editor of a consumer magazine in some ways our rival, Paige Rense of *Architectural Digest*.

The success of that first night has never lagged in subsequent years, and the Hall of Fame dinner is now firmly established as the interior design profession's most important and most glittering annual event.

But the dinner's very glitter sometimes blinds us from the fact that the Hall of Fame is more than a once-a-year celebration. It is primarily an institution of recognized excellence, and its membership, as this book is being prepared, now numbers 76 outstanding practitioners.

For several years, since the membership has grown to a substantial size and diversity, the new members have no longer been selected by the editors of *Interior Design* but have been elected by the membership itself, making the group a self-directing and self-perpetuating academy. And, true to their intended purpose, the induction dinners have raised more than half a million dollars for the accreditation work of FIDER.

What is the future of the Interior Design Magazine Hall of Fame? A glorious and active one, I believe, in which the amassed talent of its membership will be put to positive uses not now being exercised. There is a design brilliance in this group, obviously, but there is also a great deal of accumulated wisdom and experience about the profession of interior design. It will be a natural development for this wisdom and experience to be tapped for the guidance of all of the rest of us who value this most personal of all of our arts.

This book is a welcome step in that direction. Designed by Massimo Vignelli, himself a member of the Hall of Fame, it is an appropriate mirror of the depth and range and the quality of the work of these 76 designers. Seeing it all together here for the first time is an impressive experience.

And this work has a value beyond visual impressiveness. If it is true, as I believe it to be, that the brutalization of our urban environments and of our society drive us indoors for shelter, solace, refuge and beauty, then it follows that the work of the interior designer has a vital and a growing role in the maintenance of our psychological well-being. This work is not a luxury nor an indulgence; it is something that helps us function at the optimal level, something that brings (in Walter Pater's definition of art) "the highest quality to our moments as they pass," something that we all need and all deserve.

Interior design is a more serious, more demanding, more essential profession now than it has ever been before. The education of its practitioners, guided by FIDER standards, is more difficult, more extensive than it has ever been before: there is now so much to learn about how we and our interiors interact: not only about color, balance and proportion, but also about lighting, egress, ergonomics, flammability, toxicity, accessibility and environmental responsibility. The beautiful interiors that follow in this book were not formed by the simple exercise of taste or whim. They were formed by the complex exercise of a demanding profession by those judged by their peers to be that profession's masters. We salute the members of the Interior Design Magazine Hall of Fame, and we thank them.

Stanley Abercrombie
Senior Editor
Interior Design Magazine

**Selections from the
Interior Design Magazine
Hall of Fame**

Marvin B. Affrime

As founder and president of The Space Design Group, Marvin Affrime has served as a skilled interviewer, analyst, advisor, catalyst and confidant on a multitude of corporate projects. Mr. Affrime and his design partner, Frank Failla, have been able to grasp the massive functional requirements of the corporate client and weave them into original environments again and again. Many of the professional staff with whom they work are charter members of the 30-year-old firm.
One of the firm's most significant projects of the last decade was the world headquarters for International Paper in New York City, which featured an innovative public plaza and museum. More recently, the flagship facility for the advertising agency BBDO Worldwide was another prominent installation. Other projects include refurbishing all public spaces for two major office towers, the Grant Building in Pittsburgh and 130 Bloor Street in Toronto. The designers were also able to yield dramatic cost savings at new law offices for the Philadelphia headquarters of Dechert Price & Rhoads.
Residential projects include a guest house in Mt. Kisco, New York for the chairman of an international commodities company and a home in Connecticut for the managing partner of an engineering firm.
Always in pursuit of quality, The Space Design Group has twice won the 5th Avenue Association Award for architecture.

Street-level entry to the main reception area at the International Paper Company, New York City.

One of 14 general office floors at National Westminster Bank U.S.A. Work spaces are delineated with architectural ceiling and flooring treatments.

The entry to the executive area within a two-story penthouse at National Westminster Bank U.S.A.

Davis Allen

Davis Allen, a pioneer in the field of interior architecture and design, joined Skidmore, Owings and Merrill (SOM) in 1950 and quickly rose to associate partner and senior interior designer. His philosophy of total design, integrating all elements of furniture, fabrics, decorative objects and art into a single aesthetic statement expressing simplicity, refinement, and restrained luxury, became SOM's signature style.

Milestone interiors he worked on include those for Inland Steel Building (1958), the first new building in Chicago's Loop in 20 years; Chase Manhattan Plaza (1961); the Mauna Kea Beach Hotel in Hawaii (1965), which he considered the most personally satisfying project of his career; Marine Midland Bank in New York City (1967); and scores of others, including private quarters for the Lyndon Baines Johnson Library. He also designed furniture for SOM's interiors, and trained young designers who have since become leaders in the profession.

Mr. Allen received his architectural degree from Yale after studying at Brown University and traveling extensively in Europe, where he met Aalvar Alto—a decisive influence on his career. While SOM has always espoused a "team design" approach, crediting the firm rather than the individual, projects directed by Mr. Allen have received more than 50 top national and international design awards.

Dining area at Alexander & Alexander, New York City.

Overleaf: The Agnelli Suite, Tour Fiat, Paris, France.

Benjamin Baldwin

The Britanica Encyclopedia of Art lists Benjamin Baldwin as "an architect and designer of the purest, most minimal interiors...an inspirational leader in design." Born in Montgomery, Alabama, Mr. Baldwin studied painting with Hans Hoffman. He received his master of fine arts at Princeton University and attended the Cranbrook Academy of Art in Michigan. From 1939 until 1940, he worked with Eliel Saarinen and Eero Saarinen, after which he was in an architectural partnership with his brother-in-law, Harry Weese. At Skidmore, Owings and Merrill in New York from 1945 until 1947, Mr. Baldwin helped create the interior design function of the firm. He worked in independent practice on commissions for furniture, textiles, industrial, office and residential design across the country.

The sophisticated minimalist style of Mr. Baldwin's work earned him commissions with Louis Kahn for the library and dining hall at Philips Academy in Exeter, New Hampshire, 1972; with I.M. Pei, for a residence in Texas, 1969; and with Edward L. Barnes for a Minnesota residence in 1968, among others. Currently, Mr. Baldwin is working on residential projects in Florida and on furniture design for Jack Lenor Larsen, Incorporated. He recently completed a book featuring 50 years of his work in design.

In the living room of Benjamin Baldwin's Florida home, back-to-back sofas create two seating areas. All furnishings are designed by Mr. Baldwin. Bronze floor lamps are by Alberto Giacometti. Also in Mr. Baldwin's living room, walls are built out to create recesses for display shelves with concealed lighting above. Cross-legged stools are custom-made in Japan.

Louis M.S. Beal

The career of Louis M.S. Beal has been noteworthy, not only for an impressive list of projects and clients, but also for what Mr. Beal has given back to the interior design profession.

A native of Boston, he received a bachelor of science degree with honors from Rhode Island School of Design (where he now serves as a life trustee) and later studied architecture with Walter Gropius at Harvard University. From Boston, he went to New York to work for the Knoll Planning Unit for two years and then moved on to Designs for Business. There, he worked with such distinguished clients as Goldman Sachs & Company, First Boston Corporation and Time, Inc.

In 1961, Mr. Beal began what was to be an illustrious 24-year association with ISD, one of the first firms to establish itself as a commercial design specialist. At ISD, Mr. Beal was co-founder, director and executive vice president and specialized in law offices and financial and academic institutions.

Mr. Beal left ISD in 1985 to become an independent consultant. He now works on one or two projects at a time, and has collaborated with PHH/Neville Lewis, ISD and Earl Flansburgh & Associates.

As a past director of both the national and the New York Metropolitan chapter of American Society of Interior Designers; a member of the advisory board for Interior Designers for Legislation in New York; a board member for the New York Chapter of Institute of Business Designers; and an affiliate member of the Interior Designer Educators Council, Louis M.S. Beal continues to contribute his expertise and grace to the field of interior design while working on prestigious projects across the country.

The executive foyer at the Amvest Corporation, Charlottesville, Virginia (Louis M.S. Beal/ISD/Jacquelin Robertson, 1986).

Overleaf: A private dining room at the American Academy of Arts and Sciences, Cambridge, Massachusetts (Louis M.S. Beal/ISD/Kallmann, McKinnell and Wood, 1980).

Also at Amvest Corporation, Charlottesville, Virginia, the chief executive's office (Louis M.S. Beal/ISD/Jacquelin Robertson, 1986).

The executive secretary corridor at Heublin Headquarters, Hartford, Connecticut (Louis M.S. Beal/ISD/Russell, Gibson & Von Dohlin, 1974).

Joseph Braswell

The design approach of Joseph Braswell is creative and visionary. "He could very well have been a fine artist," says a friend, explaining that, "Joe can capture a vision on paper in minutes."

Mr. Braswell was born in Alabama and attended Birmingham Southern College and Parsons School of Design in New York. Having worked with Melanie Kahane, Raymond Loewy, Joseph B. Platt Associates and partner Inman Cook, he formed Braswell-Willoughby, Inc. in 1974 with Ward Willoughby. In 1990, Joseph Braswell Associates was formed.

A partial listing of Mr. Braswell's interior projects include Bergdorf Goodman and Bonwit Teller in New York; royal residences in Saudi Arabia; chalets in the Alps; corporate jets; a private steamship in Bremerhaven, Germany; retail stores and offices on Wall Street. "For me, interior design *is* an act of creation," claims Mr. Braswell. "The product is not nearly as exciting as the process."

A member of the Board of Directors of the New York Chapter of the American Society of Interior Designers (ASID), Mr. Braswell has been widely published and honored. He was presented with the ASID Designer of Distinction Award in 1989.

A human scale is maintained in a Manhattan drawing room despite its grand dimension. An antique Aubusson rug unifies the furniture arrangement.

After 50 years of neglect, this New York duplex apartment was completely reconstructed utilizing new architectural detailing, a state-of-the-art lighting program and comfortable seating.

A stainless steel chimney housing a Roman bust of Caligula dominates a Park Avenue library. Walls are covered in ultra suede and trimmed with stainless steel moldings.

Robert Bray and Michael Schaible

The work of Robert Bray and Michael Schaible is characterized by fluid lines and broad planes, giving the impression of spaciousness even in small areas.

Robert Bray and Michael Schaible began their friendship as classmates at Parsons School of Design. They continued working together at Ford and Earl Design and Saphier, Lerner, Schindler Environetics, where the majority of their experience was corporate. Together they opened Bray-Schaible in 1969 with the design of a flower shop.

Since founding the firm, they have completed projects in both the residential and commercial spectrum. Bray-Schaible does not have a "signature" look; rather, they analyze the space and evaluate the client's taste and needs to create each design. Their ability to give such individualized attention comes from their resolve to keep the firm small; support staff is never more than three, so both principals are personally involved in each installation.

Born in Ardmore, Oklahoma, Mr. Bray studied architectural engineering at Oklahoma State University. Mr. Schaible, originally from Oakley, Kansas, received his bachelor of fine arts degree from the University of Colorado. He continued his education at the Universita di Firenze per Stranieri.

Both Mr. Bray and Mr. Schaible are frequently invited to lecture at respected institutions such as the Philadelphia Museum of Art, the Rice Design Alliance and the Smithsonian Institute.

Geometric lines define the entrance to this Fifth Avenue apartment (1980).

Overleaf: The sleek dining area of a Fifth Avenue apartment in New York City (1985).

Donald Brinkmann

Donald Brinkmann, vice president and design director of Gensler and Associates/Architects, in New York, spent the first 13 years of his career as an architect with Skidmore, Owings and Merrill in San Francisco. Having moved from West to East, from architecture to interior design, he seems never to have looked back. He has brought a strong architectural orientation and a taste for "simple, good, classic/contemporary" design to the four million square feet of space he has designed for major clients: Becton Dickinson, Newsweek, Capital Bank, Nomura Securities International, and the law firm Shearman & Sterling. He has also designed a new line of furniture for Stow & Davis, and casegoods and tables for Helikon Furniture. Mr. Brinkmann's work has been published in all the important interior magazines and honored by the profession. He received the 1984 American Society of Interior Designers award for excellence in showroom design for the Hiebert showroom in Chicago; first award for executive office design from *Professional Office Design* magazine; a special judge's award from the National Glass Association for Capital Bank in Miami; and first place in the environments category of the *Annual Design Review* published by *International Design* magazine. He has also won awards for the San Paolo Bank in New York and for Goldman Sachs International, Ltd. in London from *Interiors* magazine. A graduate of the University of California at Berkeley, with a bachelor of architecture degree, he serves on Gensler's national design steering committee.

At the Capital Bank, New York City (1988), a palette of white, gray and black provides a neutral background for contemporary art and furniture.

Rich materials and minimal ornamentation form a clean design for the San Paolo Bank, New York City (1991).

A wall of gridded windows floods the reception area of Goldman Sachs International Ltd., London, England (1991) with natural light.

Thomas Britt

With residential and commercial projects worldwide, Thomas Britt designs interiors ranging from contemporary to traditional, often expertly combining styles. Along with interiors, he designs his own furnishings, which appear throughout his spaces.

Born and raised in Kansas City, Missouri, Mr. Britt studied at Parsons School of Design in New York and in the school's European program. He graduated from New York University with a bachelor of science degree. In 1959, Mr. Britt established his namesake firm in New York and began a five-year association with South American designer William Piedrahita of Bogotá, Colombia. They worked in a furniture design business with branches in New York, Texas, California and Bogotá.

Today, Mr. Britt maintains clients across the United States and in Mexico City, South America, India and Switzerland, including: Her Highness the Raj Mata of Jaipur; Princess Priya Ransit of Thailand; Ambassador Charles and Mrs. Price; Count and Countess John Forgach; Jorge Larreas of Mexico City; the Nicholas Zapatas of Mexico City, New York and Switzerland; the Fredrick Woolworths; the Clarke Swansons; and the Seymour Milsteins. In 1987, Mr. Britt received the "Giant of Interior Decorating" award from *Smithsonian* magazine. He is an honorary member of the American Society of Interior Designers.

A detail of the living room shows a Roman bust and antique engravings. The room was a winner of House Beautiful's *annual Showhouse Competition.*

Overleaf: A ballroom-turned living room features oversized sofas and 18th Century chairs arranged on a bare parquet floor.

R. Scott Bromley

R. Scott Bromley, founder of Bromley Caldari Architects, has applied his wide-range of design skills to everything from offices and museums to discos and galas. A 1963 honors graduate of McGill University's School of Architecture in Montreal, Mr. Bromley began his career with Emery Roth and later moved on to Phillip Johnson, becoming head of design at both. In 1974, he opened his own office, undertaking commissions for residences and restaurants in New York and Venezuela, industry showrooms for Alan Campbell and Beylerian, the Abitari shop—which introduced contemporary Italian furniture to New York—and Studio 54, the foremost disco of our time. Later, with partner Robin Jacobson, he designed Ralph Lauren's Polo design offices. Following Jacobson's death in 1986 from complications of AIDS, Mr. Bromley completed projects for medical offices, model apartments, residences, a Perry Ellis shoe store, and furniture for Les Prismatique and Cartier. In 1991, he entered into partnership with Jerry Caldari, undertaking the renovation and design of the Manhattan night club, Private Eyes, and design of the Charles Cowles Studios.

Mr. Bromley is a member of the American Institute of Architects (AIA). The designer of many unique galas and benefits, Mr. Bromley is the recipient of the AIA award for Abitari, the "I" Award from *Interiors* magazine, and the Lumen Award.

Three residences and the Kips Bay Boys' Club Showhouse show the scope of Mr. Bromley's talent. Lighting plays a crucial role in each design, whether it is as relaxing soft neon in the angled coves of the showhouse (opposite, upper right) or as a two-color neon "path" guiding guests through a home (opposite, upper left). Materials range from a hand-burnished, stainless steel wall in an entry (overleaf, upper left) to burl-dyed wood cabinets and black granite counters in a kitchen (opposite, lower left).

Mario Buatta

Rooms designed by Mario Buatta always delight and entertain. His sense of exuberance and showmanship may have started early—his father was a well-known orchestra leader in New York.

Translating English country decoration into attractive interiors in America has been his forté since launching his own business 26 years ago. A passion for collecting antique furniture and objects has enriched work for clients that include Barbara Walters, Charlotte Ford, and Billy Joel. His appreciation for period styles has led to projects such as the executive offices of the Metropolitan Opera House; galleries of the Henry Francis DuPont Winterthur Museum; and Blair House.

Mr. Buatta studied architecture at Cooper Union and attended Parsons School of Design in Paris. He lectures extensively, is a member of the American Society of Interior Designers, and serves on a number of boards. He chaired the Winter Antique Show sponsored by East Side Settlement for 15 years.

Now Mr. Buatta's special eye for design is enlivening a series of collections of products for the house that bear his name—furniture, bed and bath linens, lamps, china, fabrics and wallcoverings. (He is often referred to as the "Prince of Chintz.") These products reinforce his philosophy that "interiors should be colorful, comfortable, timeless, and above all, personal."

One side of an English country bedroom; drapes are trimmed in rope and ruffles to enhance the look.

Overleaf: Sunlight beckons visitors to this vignette in an elegant living room.

Richard A. Carlson

Richard A. Carlson is principal-in-charge of interior design at the New York-based Swanke Hayden Connell Associates (SHCA) and is currently serving his second term as president of the New York Chapter of the Institute of Business Designers (IBD). In the four years that Mr. Carlson has led the New York Chapter of IBD, he has aided in the development of programs such as Pioneers of Design honoring those who have helped establish the profession. The chapter was a leader in creating environmental programs such as the S.E.E.D. newsletter and the first environmental round table for major manufacturers and designers. Mr. Carlson sees IBD as an educator in the growing interior design profession. Before SHCA, he worked with Carson, Lundin & Shaw. Mr. Carlson received his bachelor of fine arts degree from Pratt Institute and went on to post-graduate studies in architecture and interiors at Lincoln College at Oxford University in England. He is an associate member of the American Institute of Architects.

Mr. Carlson's expertise in designing corporate facilities has come from years of experience. He has supervised projects including the American Express Company, Dow Jones & Company, Prudential-Bache Securities, and Lloyd's Bank Securities of New York; the law offices of Coudert Brothers in New York, and Steel Hector & Davis in West Palm Beach, Florida; and the corporate offices of the Northwestern Mutual Life Insurance Company in Milwaukee, Wisconsin and RJR Nabisco in New York.

Richard Carlson received the Ron Wallin Distinguished Merit Award from IBD.

The reception area at SHCA Headquarters, New York City (1990).

Another view of the reception area at SHCA Headquarters, New York City (1990).

Wood tones create a subdued atmosphere in the library of American Express, World Financial Center, New York City (1986).

Customer dining at American Express, World Financial Center, New York City (1986).

Steve Chase

Certain by age 17 that his career lay in design, Steve Chase sought formal training at the Rhode Island School of Design and the Art Center College of Design. From there he went on to work in Geneva with William P. Lear on various design projects including the initial interior concepts for the Lear jet.

A 14-year affiliation with Arthur Elrod Associates in Palm Springs followed, of which during the last six years Mr. Chase was vice-president. In 1980 he established Steve Chase Associates in Rancho Mirage, California. Stirred by the geometry, volume and texture of contemporary architecture, Mr. Chase prefers to work closely with the architect from the outset of any design project. He departs from the very formal and the very traditional, and stresses strong forms expressed in elements from nature—stone, wood, leather—all chosen to blend luxury with comfort and sculptural statement. "The temple was a place where people went for spiritual inspiration. For me, architecture fulfills this purpose." Although the West Coast provides the sites for the preponderance of Mr. Chase's work, he and his staff have a worldwide reputation. Aircraft, yachts and homes in locales as distant as Germany bear his hallmark.

His national and international projects include work for Christopher Hemmeter of Hawaii and Colorado; Kenneth Behring of San Francisco and Danville, California; the Kwee family of Singapore and Beverly Hills; and for the Bob Hope Cultural Center.

The master bedroom in a Northern California home typifies Steve Chase's architectural interests.

Strong architectural lines and artwork define the living room of this Laguna Beach, California residence.

At the Luten Clarey Stern Showroom, the space was stripped down to expose the skeleton and structure of the room, providing a unique backdrop for traditional furnishings.

Beginning with research at the local library, the restoration and renovation of this 1890s Connecticut residence lasted two years.

During restoration, the bones of the Connecticut home were maintained while rendering it appropriate for a family of six to live in comfortably.

Barbara D'Arcy

"As Barbara D'Arcy goes, so goes the nation," wrote *The New York Times* when Ms. D'Arcy was Bloomingdale's fashion director of home furnishings.

Born and raised in New York City, Ms. D'Arcy majored in art and decoration (including architectural and structural design) at the College of New Rochelle in New York. After college, she joined the Clara Dudley workshop of the Alexander Smith Carpet Company, where she remained until 1952.

Ms. D'Arcy began her career at Bloomingdale's in 1953 as an assistant to Henriette Granville. Since then, her responsibilities have included merchandise display, furniture design and supervision of the model rooms that the store presents four times a year.

In 1973, she became director of merchandise presentation, which included all stores and carried the responsibility for the total look of Bloomingdale's throughout the country.

Ms. D'Arcy was appointed vice president in 1978. Today, she maintains a hectic schedule as senior vice president and director of merchandise planning.

A member of the American Society of Interior Designers, the National Home Fashions League and the Decorators Club, Ms. D'Arcy has been included in the *Who's Who of American Women* and the *Who's Who in Commerce and Industry*. She and her husband, a furniture designer, live in New York City and share an enthusiasm for opera, theater, museums and antique hunting.

Soft ivory seating, a curtained bed and green walls make this master suite an enticing retreat.

The main floor
at Bloomingdale's,
New York City

The 1972 Bloomingdale's
Centennial Celebration.
Complete lattice gazebo with
clear Plexiglas lit from behind
is in background.

...demonstrating the range over which Ms. D'Arcy is skilled, an inviting bedroom featuring an Empire daybed and a desk clad in brass. Flooring is of white marble.

...innovative corrugated cardboard furniture designed by Barbara D'Arcy.

Orlando Diaz-Azcuy

As head of his own design studio, Orlando Diaz-Azcuy Designs, Inc., and formerly as design principal for Gensler and Associates/Architects, Mr. Diaz-Azcuy has had a far-reaching influence on the field of interior design. While with Gensler, he established his reputation for subtlety, sophistication, and simplicity with projects such as the Levi Strauss and Company headquarters in San Francisco; the United Bank of Denver's headquarters; the Los Angeles showroom for Steelcase; and Marvin Davis, and Jessica McClintock in Los Angeles and the international terminal of the San Francisco airport.

In 1985, he opened his own design studio and produced lines of furniture and textiles for Hickory Business Furniture. Both collections received *Contract* magazine's Charles S. Gelber Award as "Best of Competition" in 1986. Further work completed under his direction includes Shearman & Sterling in San Francisco; Yomitan Hotel in Japan and several projects for Western Athletic Clubs, Inc.

Mr. Diaz-Azcuy received his bachelor of arts in architecture from Catholic University of America in Washington, D.C. and his master's degrees in landscape architecture and city and regional planning from the University of California at Berkeley. He teaches summer sessions at the Harvard Graduate School of Design.

In 1982 Orlando Diaz-Azcuy was designated "Designer of the Year" by *Interiors* magazine.

In the passageway between the reception area and Orlando Diaz-Azcuy's office and presentation room in San Francisco, mirrored ceiling and walls create the illusion of endless space.

The designer's office and presentation room in San Francisco house a 19th century Chinese bed, an all leather screen and rainbow chairs designed by Orlando Diaz-Azcuy.

The reception room and view of conference room at the San Francisco offices of Orlando Diaz-Azcuy Design. The two Chalice chairs in gold are from the collection designed by Orlando Diaz-Azcuy.

At the Bostwick & Tehin Law Offices, San Francisco, a contemporary design has the richness of old Italian finishes and colors. Lawyers' corridors with slanted walls create bookshelves and work stations on the opposite side.

Angelo Donghia

Following the creed that, "First of all, I design for the people," Angelo Donghia created interiors ranging from public places such as the salons and staterooms of the S.S. Norway to the intimate ambience of his own Manhattan townhouse. His award-winning sheets and towels for J.P. Stevens, his collection of wallcoverings and fabrics for James Seeman Studios, his upholstered furniture and tables for Kroehler, and coordinated lines of dinnerware, barware, giftware and accessories all had a profound impact on the American marketplace. Barbara Walters, Ralph Lauren, Diana Ross, Mary Tyler Moore and Halston were among Mr. Donghia's many residential clients. In the contract field, he completed the world headquarters of Pepsico, Inc.; the Opera Club at the Metropolitan Opera; the Glen Oaks Golf and Country Club; and the Omni Hotels in Miami and Atlanta.

Mr. Donghia was born in Vandergrift, Pennsylvania and educated at Parsons School of Design. In 1968, he started Vice Versa, now Donghia Textiles. Donghia Associates, specializing in residential and contract interior design, was established two years later. Soon Donghia Showrooms opened to the trade across the country. The establishment of Donghia Furniture marked the beginning of his made-to-order furniture line. The continued success of his companies despite his tragic death in 1985 indicates not only Mr. Donghia's exceptional taste, but also his tremendous business acumen.

Lacquered green walls, a silver papered ceiling and bleached floors wrap the living room of a Manhattan townhouse in crisp serenity.

Henry End

Henry End was born in England and received his design training at the Royal College of Art in London. He spent six years with the Royal Air Force before coming to the United States as a motion picture set designer for productions for Warner Brothers, Twentieth Century Fox and Universal. Since 1948, he has built a reputation as a successful interior designer.

With offices in Miami and London, Henry End Associates produces interior, environmental, graphic and product design for a variety of clients, but the firm's area of expertise is in planning hotels, restaurants, condominium apartments, offices and educational and transportational facilities.

In addition to projects around the world, Mr. End has written various books on design. The *Saturday Review* reviewed his first text, *Interiors Book of Hotel and Motor Hotels*, "Design is a serious topic...we have a certain gratitude for the testimony of a practitioner such as Henry End. He is something of an expert in popular taste, and his book has been assembled with something like the devotion that Mr. End spends on his profession."

Mr. End is a member of the American Society of Interior Designers. He has received several awards and his work has appeared in many exhibitions.

The lounge in the Hyatt Regency Hotel of Miami, Florida.

The lobby at the Palm Bay Hotel in Miami, Florida.

Billy W. Francis

While many designers blend antiques with contemporary furnishings, Billy Francis has a special eye for selecting the best of different periods and styles. When mixing the old and the new, he claims, "The exact balance depends on the client...but the aim is always quality, and above all, comfort. Within this framework, I can also concentrate on providing the exquisite details that my clients and I demand." He labels his look as "classical comfort."

Mr. Francis began his design education with graduate study at the New York School of Interior Design. He founded his own practice in Houston in 1972 and in 1986, opened his New York offices. Although his reputation is that of "Houston's society designer," his domestic interiors can be found in California, Florida, Acapulco and London. His focus is on residential work, but he has designed commercial interiors for clients as well.

Before establishing his own firm, Mr. Francis was associated with Lord & Taylor in New York; Wellington Hall and Wilds and Canon Design in Houston.

Billy Francis is a member of the International Society of Interior Designers.

Custom-made panels recalling antique frescos and a hand-painted floor emphasize the neo-classical mood of this space.

All elements in the design of this home were selected to complement and enhance the client's extensive collection of paintings.

Contemporary backgrounds with classical allusions create a magnificent setting for a collection of neo-classical objects and furnishings.

M. Arthur Gensler, Jr.

Arthur Gensler is the founding principal and president of Gensler and Associates/Architects. Over the past 26 years, he has built an international practice with more than 600 employees in eight offices in the United States and abroad.

Mr. Gensler opened his firm in 1965 with the belief that interior architectural design, space planning and programming are distinct yet tightly integrated services that clients need from a traditional architectural firm. Gensler and Associates/Architects has been ranked consistently as a top design firm by *Interior Design* magazine.

Involved in administration, Mr. Gensler has participated in the design of key projects including: the Moscone Convention Center expansion in San Francisco; Delta Airlines Terminal at Los Angeles International Airport; Levi Strauss Corporate Headquarters in San Francisco; King Fahd International Airport in Saudi Arabia; and Bank of America Plaza in New York City.

Mr. Gensler actively participates in the education of other architects and serves as a member advisor to several universities. He has taught at the University of California at Berkeley, the University of Arizona, Arizona State and Cornell University. He also co-authored *A Rational Approach to Office Planning*.

A founding member of the National American Institute of Architects (AIA) Committee on Interior Architecture, Mr. Gensler was elected to AIA Fellowship status in 1980.

Support columns wrapped in mirror-polished stainless steel reflect the movement of light and color at the United Airlines Union Square ticket office, San Francisco, California.

Overleaf: A sophisticated environment provides the setting for an art collection and projects national image of the law offices of Brown & Bain, Phoenix, Arizona (1989).

Margo Grant

Margo Grant, vice president and managing principal of Gensler and Associates/Architects, joined Gensler's Houston office in 1973 after 13 years with Skidmore, Owings and Merrill in San Francisco. In 1979, with a staff of two, she opened Gensler's New York office. Going after—and winning—major commissions in the East Coast market, Ms. Grant built it into a high profile entity with a staff of 130 and a client roster of over 80, including such leading corporate and legal organizations as Mobil Oil, Morgan Bank, Goldman Sachs, Newsweek, Cadwalader Wickersham & Taft, Davis Polk & Wardwell. In 1989, she opened Gensler's London office.

Born on Montana's Blackfoot Indian Reservation, Ms. Grant graduated summa cum laude from the University of Oregon with bachelor of science and bachelor of interior architecture degrees. She has received many design awards and was featured in *The New York Times, Women in Design,* and *Crain's New York Business.* Ms. Grant is a member of the Institute of Business Designers.

"By sheer force of her personality and talents, she has established Gensler as a leading design firm in the city," says an outside colleague. "She is a formidable woman whose staff, without exception, credits her with providing the best learning experience because she takes such great interest in her work."

A library on the top two floors overlooks a ten-story atrium at the law offices of Cadwalader, Wickersham & Taft, New York City (1985).

The law offices of King & Spalding, Atlanta, Georgia are based on a strong planning concept (1991).

Covington & Burling, Washington, D.C. (1981 and 1988). The angularity of the building presented a challenge in achieving the client's goal of a traditional law office. Art, antique and oriental rug collections are central to public spaces on each floor.

Michael Graves

From his offices in Princeton, New Jersey, Michael Graves has conceived of everything from a master plan for the Detroit Institute of Arts to furniture for Atelier International, Arkitektura and Dunbar to tabletop accessories.

Mr. Graves is closely associated with post-modernism and believes that people make natural associations with color, form and composition. His hallmark, a strong muted color palette, has influenced design across the spectrum. He often weaves symbolic elements into his work.

Born in Indianapolis, Mr. Graves received his bachelor of science degree in architecture from the University of Cincinnati and a master of architecture from Harvard. He was a 1960 winner of the Rome Prize in Architecture and served as a Fellow at the American Academy in Rome, where he is now a trustee. He established the firm bearing his name in Princeton in 1964.

With a staff of more than 80 professionals, Mr. Graves is the principal designer for all of his firm's projects. Among them are the Portland Building; Riverbend Music Center in Cincinnati; the Clos Pegase Winery in Napa Valley; the Walt Disney World Dolphin and Swan Hotels; the Whitney Museum of American Art; and stores for Lenox China. He remains personally involved throughout each installation.

Mr. Graves has garnered 15 *Progressive Architecture* awards, eight national American Institute of Architects Honor Awards, and the American Academy and Institute of Arts and Letters' Arnold W. Brunner Memorial Prize in Architecture in 1980. Exhibitions of his work span the globe, from Denver to Tokyo to Paris to Mexico City to New York.

The reading room at the San Juan Capistrano Library in California.

The Swan Fountain Lobby at the Walt Disney World Swan Hotel, Lake Buena Vista, Florida.

The Main Lobby at the Aventine, La Jolla, California.

The ground floor rotunda at The Team Disney Building, Burbank, California.

Bruce Gregga

Bruce Gregga's sense of style has made him the "designer of choice" for some of Chicago's most gracious homes and commercial interiors. Before opening his firm in 1970, Mr. Gregga worked in advertising and photographic design. The experience helped train him to see the value of mixing traditional and modern elements and techniques for working with color and texture. Today, Bruce Gregga Interiors has 20 to 30 projects in progress at any given time.

Along with residences in Chicago, New York and London, Mr. Gregga's projects include the Whitehall Hotel; Ultimo, a retail specialty clothing store; the Standard Club; McDonald's Restaurants and the corporate office of a multi-franchise McDonald's Restaurant owner; and the lobby of the Watertower Condominiums. Mr. Gregga has served on the Formica Corporation Design Advisory Board and as a judge for the Resources Council Annual Product Design Awards Competition. He is a professional member of the American Society of Interior Designers; of the Cooper Hewitt Museum Decorative Arts Advisory Committee; and of the Smithsonian Institution's National Museum of Design.

Among his many honors, Bruce Gregga was named the "Dean of Design" by the Chicago Design Sources for the Merchandise Mart, and was a speaker at "*Architectural Digest* at the Smithsonian", a lecture series featuring celebrated international interior designers.

A Lucas Samara wire sculpture, along with a pair of Ed Paschke paintings and a blue glass vase by Dan Dailey, are points of focus in the design of this Chicago apartment's living room.

Overleaf: Mr. Gregga's careful selection of color and materials form an ideal setting for artwork in the same apartment's dining room. Horses are Deborah Butterfield; Dale Chihuly glass and William Morris vase are on the buffet.

Charles Gwathmey and Robert Siegel

"Our designs are a result of our interaction, which is intense, self-critical, questioning, yet always supportive. We share common beliefs and we motivate each other to extend beyond our individual capabilities."

Charles Gwathmey attended the University of Pennsylvania School of Architecture and received his master of architecture degree from Yale University. There, he was awarded the William Wirt Winchester Fellowship and a Fulbright Grant. Earning his bachelor of architecture degree from Pratt Institute, Robert Siegel received his master of architecture degree from Harvard University. Since establishing Gwathmey Siegel & Associates Architects in 1968, the pair have designed and constructed both commercial and residential buildings and interiors.

The pair's most recent accomplishment is at the Frank Lloyd Wright-designed Guggenheim in New York City where they renovated the existing facility and created an addition to house the museum's permanent collection. They have been credited with restoring the original intent of Wright's design as well as improving upon it with the addition.

They have appeared in a multitude of books and publications in the field. Mr. Gwathmey and Mr. Siegel's awards roster includes National American Institute of Architects Honor Awards for the Straus Residence in Purchase, New York; for Whig Hall at Princeton University; for the dormitory, dining and student union facility at the State University College at Purchase, New York; and for the Taft Residence in Cincinnati, Ohio.

SBK Entertainment World, Inc., New York City (1986). The 42,000 sq. ft. offices of this music publishing and movie production company are centered around a two-story reception area and stairway.

Overleaf: Gwathmey apartment, New York City (1988-90). A typical 2,500 sq. ft. Fifth Avenue apartment was transformed into a spatially complex "pavilion loft" featuring custom-designed furniture.

Albert Hadley

Interiors that reflect strong personalities are what Albert Hadley strives for. Through the years, he has created scores of attractive rooms for eminent clients with the sure hand of a man well-educated in his craft.

Mr. Hadley was born in Nashville and feels his early life in the south has influenced his work. Arriving in New York just after World War II, he attended Parsons School of Design for three years, and after teaching there for five years, joined the design firm of McMillen.

In 1963, he formed a partnership with Mrs. Henry Parish II. The firm of Parish-Hadley Associates enjoys a worldwide reputation for designing interiors that are highly individual, and for such clients as Mrs. Annette de la Renta, Ambassador and Mrs. Henry Grunwald, and Mr. Glenn Bernbaum. A talent for creating handsome, welcoming spaces has also brought them commissions for executive offices, hotels and other public places. Hadley-designed interiors often seem very sculptural because of his attention to architecture, and the way he arranges furniture and art. He is a master at using subtle contrasts that lead to a clarity of design that is his trademark.

Mr. Hadley has been quoted as saying, "I'm not interested so much in the museum quality of an object as I am in its integrity and aesthetic dynamics. I like things that are a reflection of a passionate and cultivated taste, a knowledgeable eye."

Sheer linen Austrian shades allow natural light into the library of Mrs. Vincent Astor. Contemporary furniture is covered in chintz and red raw silk; Bessarabian carpet.

Overleaf: Silver leaf iron table topped with a 1930s ball echoes walls sheathed in silver tea paper and mirrored cornice in Mr. Hadley's apartment.

Mark Hampton

A great love of architecture and the decorative arts, past and present, has been an important key to the design work of Mark Hampton. Many of his commissions are a result of his keen interest in restoration and preservation, and include the White House, Blair House, the Naval Observatory (the official residence of the Vice President of the United States in Washington, D.C.), the Metropolitan Museum of Art, Gracie Mansion and the National Academy of Design in New York. He has designed interiors for offices, hotels, clubs, railroad cars, airplanes and boats. Currently he is using his talents to create a special collection for the Hickory Chair Company of historically inspired furniture that is available in stores across the country. Mr. Hampton's academic credentials include DePauw University, the London School of Economics, and a masters degree from the New York University Institute of Fine Arts. Before opening his own firm in 1976, he worked with David Hicks, Mrs. Henry Parish II and McMillen.

His book, *Mark Hampton on Decorating*, is a best seller. In the introduction he writes that decorating has to do with people and beauty, peace and pleasure, and the timeless activities of domestic life. His latest book, *Legendary Decorators of the 20th Century*, edited by Jacqueline Onassis for Doubleday, has just been published. He is in the Best Dressed Hall of Fame. Mr. Hampton is married to Duane Hampton and is the father of two grown daughters.

Mark Hampton

The walls of a double-height Fifth Avenue drawing room overlooking Central Park are upholstered in wool damask; cabinetry is mahogany. The room is a powerful background for collections of books and objéts d'art.

Overleaf: The woods, red walls and glints of brass and gold create a subdued Edwardian atmosphere in the library of a New York townhouse, which can also be used for dining.

Another view of the Fifth Avenue drawing room shows custom-made bookcases filled with the client's collection of first editions on either side of an English marble mantel; Axminster rug is Persian.

David Hicks

With the trained eye of a painter and sculptor, David Hicks moved easily into the world of design in the early 1950s, and with a profound effect. His work and his books on decoration gave him a worldwide reputation early in his career. Now, projects range from Buckingham Palace and houses in the English countryside to apartments and houses throughout Europe and America.

His great sense of color, proportion, and history have enlivened film sets, restaurants, hotels, government residences and many simple products for the house. "His brilliant small-patterned carpets revolutionized the floors of the world," wrote Billy Baldwin in his book *Billy Baldwin Decorates*.

Mr. Hicks, born in 1929, educated at Charterhouse and the London Central School of Arts and Crafts, has spent a lifetime observing and establishing style. In his book, *On Living with Taste,* he writes: "I am convinced that taste, whether it is good or bad, personal or impersonal, is formed by looking. It is only a matter of being sufficiently aware and interested, and of training your eye to look at things clearly and ruthlessly. It is never the value of objects or pictures placed together in the same room, or the quality of furniture which is used that gives style and which shows taste. It is their selection and the way they are put together."

One of his current focuses is on garden design. His exceptional talents are challenging nature to produce its best with style and taste.

At the South Portico, square and circular Doric columns contrast and outer walls are faced with concrete made of local sand, stone and terra cotta fragments.

Natural Artists canvas spans the walls of this two story living room. Designed by Mr. Hicks, the carpet was specially woven; a bust of George II sits on a Queen Anne "violet de brèche" chimney piece.

Richard Himmel

A specialist in residential design with offices based in Chicago and Palm Beach, Richard Himmel also produces noted design work for hotels, country clubs, retail stores, banks, railroad cars and restaurants.

He has designed upholstered furniture for Dods-Murdick Transitional Furniture, Baker Furniture Company and Interior Crafts, Incorporated. Other project credits include the Playboy Club and Resort in Lake Geneva, Wisconsin; Marbury Place Hotel in Washington, D.C.; and installations for The Limited clothing store chain.

Most recently he completed an original collection of soft seating for his showrooms located in Chicago's Merchandise Mart, and has also opened an antique gallery to complement his design atelier.

Acclaimed author of 14 novels, Mr. Himmel studied at the University of Chicago under the tutelage of Thornton Wilder. In addition to his work as an interior designer, he is also a book critic for the *Chicago Sun Times*. Mr. Himmel is the past president of the Midwest Chapter of the American Society of Interior Designers (ASID) and received the 1982 Euster Award for outstanding contributions to the interior design industry. He was named an ASID Fellow at the 1988 National Congress in Boston. In 1987, the Chicago design community bestowed its Dean of Design Award to Mr. Himmel. In 1992, the ASID presented him with the Designer of Distinction Award.

The dining room overlooking the lake front at Mr. Himmel's Chicago residence. Melrose House gold leaf Regency chairs surround a "draped" dining table of his design.

Detail of Mr. Himmel's Palm Beach living room showing a scarlet japanned Louis XV commode. 18th Century brackets holding antique Japanese figures flank artwork by Max Ernst and Jean Dubuffet.

An antique lacquered "House God" on an 18th Century Chinese lacquer armoire in the Palm Beach living room overlooks a Louis XV bergère and a kidney reading table signed by Latz.

In Mr. Himmel's Palm Beach library, bookcases display his collection of card plates. A 50s game table by Hagnauer and a carved table by Edgar Brandt complete the visual treat.

Another area of the library exhibits work by Adolf Gottlieb and Marino Marini. Red lacquer Anglo-Indian chairs of carved teak and a demi-lune console are below.

Howard Hirsch

Credited with revolutionizing the field of hotel design as a professional discipline, Howard Hirsch is founder and chairman of Hirsch/Bedner Associates (HBA) of Santa Monica, California, the largest firm in the world specializing in hotel design.

HBA develops a unique understanding of the geographic, cultural, and financial requirements that facilitate worthy design and operational profitability for each hotel they plan.

Mr. Hirsch attended Chicago's Art Institute and is a graduate of the Sorbonne and the Ecole des Beaux Arts. His extensive travels in the Far East when he first pursued a career as an artist and designer led him to form a lifelong fascination with the Orient which is reflected in his firm's prominent use of antiques and contemporary Asian art.

Dramatic stage settings in public areas, museum quality art featured as an accent or a collection, atrium lobbies with fountains or waterfalls, creatively unexpected lighting, and the introduction of the fine European-style residential hotel to the United States are all HBA innovations.

Mr. Hirsch was the first western designer to work in the People's Republic of China where he created the White Swan Hotel interiors in Guangzhou (Canton) which has proved both a tourist and native Chinese attraction. Other recent projects include: Hyatt Regencies in Aruba, Kaui, Belgrade and Perth; the Kanazawa Ana Hotel in Japan; and the Churchill Bar & Brasserie in London.

In 1986, the Conrad Hilton, Chicago, Illinois, was reopened following a major renovation and restoration of some of the most magnificent rooms in the country. Shown here is the Normandy Lounge, a pre-function space for the Grand Ballroom.

Overleaf: The Peninsula Hotel of New York, built in 1906, was reopened in 1988. A curving alabaster stairway covered in hand-woven carpet graces the entry. The ornamental ceiling was the only element salvageable from the original structure.

The Grand Hyatt Hong Kong Hotel opened in 1989. High ceilings, large marble columns and sweeping symmetrical stairways create a lobby in the tradition of the great dramatic hotels of Europe and Asia.

William Hodgins

Concentrating on residential interiors, William Hodgins has a reputation for crafting individual, inviting and elegant spaces from Boston to Palm Beach to California.

Mr. Hodgins uses intense color sparingly; he prefers creamy palettes accented with rich textures. He once told *House Beautiful*, "I work very hard to bring a sense of light into rooms, and pale shades are the best way to do that." The warmth that seems to emanate from Mr. Hodgins' rooms, even those with the most elaborate antiques and accessories, is a trademark. "Simplicity may be one reason that people feel comfortable," he says.

Mr. Hodgins was born in Canada and received his degree from Parsons School of Design in New York. His first job in the field was with the offices of Parish Hadley Associates, where he spent five years. In 1968, he relocated to Boston and established his namesake firm. Today, from his offices in a historic Back Bay townhouse, he works with a roster of loyal clients including, among others, the Taubmans, the Goulds, the Royhatyns, the Bernons and the Cables.

Mr. Hodgins is a member of the Board of Governors at the Tufts New England Medical Center and of Hospice West.

A sun-filled corner of a bedroom in a Boston home.

Work area in a summer home surrounded by tall trees and a garden.

A small dining room has old world charm.

Florence Knoll Bassett

Florence Knoll Bassett, co-founder of the Knoll Planning Unit, was one of a handful of visionary designers who led America into the International Style. Born Florence Schust in Michigan and educated at Kingswood School and Cranbrook Academy of Art, as a young woman she was virtually adopted into the family of the influential Finnish architect Eliel Saarinen. Later she studied with Ludwig Mies van der Rohe at the Illinois Institute of Technology.

According to magazine editor (and Hall of Fame Special Award recipient) Olga Gueft, "There was a moment in which nothing that was being done in American furniture or interiors was relevant or appropriate. She was conscious that there was a vacuum to be filled. Something about her life is very charged, very electric."

By 1957, the Knoll Planning Unit had amassed an important record of interior design installations including the Connecticut General Life Insurance Company at Hartford, the first open modular plan office of its kind. There were also projects for Alcoa, CBS, The Dow Chemical Company Institute for Advanced Study and several projects around the world for the U.S. State Department. As Florence Knoll was designing interiors, she was also developing furniture designed to meet the needs of these companies. She retired to private life in 1965. The prestigious list of honors and awards earned by Florence Knoll Bassett include those presented by the Museum of Modern Art, American Institute of Decorators, Center for the Advanced Study of Behavioral Sciences and the American Institute of Architects.

CBS Headquarters, New York City (1964). President Frank Stanton's office suite is timeless in its simple sophistication.

Sarah Tomerlin Lee

"In days when E.R.A. meant 'earned run average' to some and 'Emergency Relief Administration' to fewer still, Sarah Tomerlin Lee was already staking out her share of equal rights in competitive fields," wrote *Interior Design* magazine when Sarah Tomerlin Lee was inducted into the Hall of Fame.

Mrs. Lee was born in Union City, Tennessee and educated at Randolph-Macon Woman's College in Lynchburg, Virginia, where she is now a trustee emeritus. She held editorial positions at *Vogue* and *Harper's Bazaar* before being appointed editor-in-chief of *House Beautiful*. Later, she became vice president of Lord & Taylor in charge of "creativity" (advertising display, promotion and public relations). In 1971, her husband died, and she "temporarily" took over his design firm, Tom Lee Ltd., beginning her third and current career.

Under Mrs. Lee's leadership, the firm's project list has grown to include the Helmsley Palace, the Bellevue in Philadelphia, the Willard Inter-Continental Hotel in Washington and 40 other major hotels in the United States as well as resorts, inns and luxury apartment buildings.

Mrs. Lee's work has been featured in *Interior Design, Interiors,* as well as *Crain's New York, Fortune, The New York Times* and others. She is a founding member of the N.Y. Landmarks Conservancy, a member of the American Society of Interior Designers, the Decorator's Club and the New York School of Interior Design.

Le Parker Meridien's 57th Street Promenade, New York City, takes full advantage of its eccentric 16 foot wide, 100 foot long corridor to the central lobby with mirrors and a mosaic ceiling 60 feet above a medieval floor.

The Barrymore Lounge atop the historic Bellevue of Philadelphia features views of the city and murals on a vaulted ceiling.

Luminous Italian garden murals and light colors give the Doral Park Avenue Saturnia Dining Room a feeling of spaciousness despite the low space.

Naomi Leff

Naomi Leff is recognized as a premier specialist in retail design. Since the inception of Naomi Leff and Associates in 1980, she has established the consummate store image for such clients as Saks Fifth Avenue; Ferragamo; Gucci; Holt Renfrew; Polo Ralph Lauren and Giorgio Armani. "Being a designer," she says, "means listening to your clients, seeing their vision and then interpreting." Acclaimed for her innovative A/X Armani Exchange Shops, she has also successfully translated Giorgio Armani's Milan look into Boston's elegant Collection Boutique. She has also won accolades for her painstaking renovation of Ralph Lauren's Rhinelander Mansion in New York. Although she is noted for her work in the retail arena, her client roster also boasts diverse and prestigious projects for Grammercy Capital Management Corporation, Metromedia 5 and Burlington Northern Railroad.

Ms. Leff earned her bachelor of science degree at the State University of New York at Cortland. At the University of Wisconsin, she completed a master's program in sociology and she received a master of science degree in environmental design at Pratt Institute. She worked with John Carl Warnecke/Eleanor LeMaire Associates and was a senior designer at Bloomingdale's before founding her namesake firm in 1980.

In 1988, Ms. Leff was elected to the Board of Directors of the Fashion Group, Inc. She was given the Distinguished Alumni Award at Pratt Institute in 1990 and in 1991 was nominated to the Board of Trustees. She has earned numerous other citations as well.

The corridor at the Polo Ralph Lauren store, New York is intimate and sophisticated.

Ms. Leff helped further the classic image of Polo Ralph Lauren stores in Beverly Hills.

Men's shoes at the Giorgio
Armani Collection in Boston.

Neville Lewis

Neville Lewis founded his New York based firm in 1976 with four people and turned it into an organization with 180. He attributes his success to a very basic approach. "I believe in good design, but it has to be human, and it has to be appropriate," he says. Neville Lewis Associates enjoyed many long-term relationships, designing headquarters for ARCO and IBM's Royal Tech Center in Dallas, and offices for Dean Witter Reynolds, Drexel Burnham Lambert, and Smith Barney. Mr. Lewis received a bachelor of fine arts degree in interior design from Syracuse University and a Certificate in Industrial Design from Pratt Institute. In his early career he did product design for Becker & Becker and Raymond Loewy, and office design for Michael Saphier Associates and Morganelli-Heumann. In 1987, Lewis' firm was acquired by PHH Group, and more recently by Hellmuth Obata Kassabaum. He remains active in the profession, consulting, serving on various boards, lecturing and writing.

Mr. Lewis is a member of the Institute of Business Designers (IBD). He has won many design and service awards, from IBD, the American Society of Interior Designers and others. His projects and writings have been published in the design press, and his firm has been written about in *The New York Times*, *Newsweek* and *Crain's New York Business*.

Neville Lewis

An art collection was a significant force in the design of Burlington Northern, as seen in this view of the reception area.

Overleaf: Neville Lewis' personal art collection and books are on center stage in the living and dining area of his New York apartment.

Robert Metzger

Robert Metzger was born and raised in New York City. Following graduation from New York University, he embarked on a career in investment and analysis on Wall Street. But after extensive travel abroad, he decided to try his hand at decorating and design and began study at the New York School of Interior Design.

He seems to have made the right decision. Mr. Metzger began work at Past and Present, a firm where he gained a knowledge and appreciation of antiques which are integral in each of his designs. Since 1973, he has been president of Robert Metzger Interiors. Having appeared frequently in numerous international journals and national publications, Mr. Metzger has developed a reputation for design that is classic and fresh, no matter what the setting. He works both overseas and in the States on commercial and residential projects. His talents now are directed to furniture, fabric for Fabriyaz and bed linens by Bibb for Royalton.

A member of the American Society of Interior Designers, Mr. Metzger has lectured at many organizations including the Smithsonian Institute in Washington, D.C.

The classic entryway to Robert Metzger's offices in New York City displays male and female figures purchased in Paris. Walls are trompe l'oeil done in stone to look like sienna marble.

Antiques blended with contemporary pieces create excitement in this dining room. Jean Sene table is done in lacquer linen; chandelier is directoire, tole and crystal.

"My office is like sitting in someone's library or living room," says Robert Metzger of his New York office. An eclectic mix tied together by color features a desk made from the base of an American pool table with an Italian Intarsia top.

Juan Montoya

"A room does not need to be filled. Rather, I look at the room to see what it has to offer and what I can do to enhance it. Eccentricity is always preferable to the bland and safe."

Juan Montoya first studied architecture at Universitad Gran Colombia in his native Bogotá before coming to New York to earn a design degree at Parsons School of Design. He began his career at Ford and Earl Design in New York and later worked in Paris and Milan. In 1978, he founded Montoya Design Corporation, and in 1988, Juan Montoya Furniture & Accessories. He has also opened in "Formentera" Bogotá, a retail store carrying unique art, antiques and furnishings.

Mr. Montoya's commercial interior projects include Barney's New York Apparel Store, the Christian Dior and Jones of New York showrooms, and the offices of United Features Syndicate, Inc. In the residential realm, he has designed the homes of artist Fernando Botero, producer Mario Kassarand and many others. He has designed Kips Bay Decorator Showhouses and works on restoration and design projects from Venezuela to New Jersey. The 1977 and 1980 Hexter Awards for Interior of the Year; three Roscoe Awards; listings in the *Who's Who in the East*; appearances on CNN and lectures at Parsons School of Design, the New York School of Interior Design and the Fashion Institute of Technology exemplify the respect Mr. Montoya has earned in the design profession.

The offices of Juan Montoya Design Corporation in New York City.

Overleaf: Also at the New York offices of the designer, the reception area.

Frank Nicholson

The name of Frank Nicholson, principal of his own design firm in Concord, Massachusetts, is synonymous with luxury hotel design. His design philosophy is to bring a timeless, classically enduring quality of design to top-of-the-market hotels while featuring fine art and antiques in a residential scale, and to ensure that each hotel reflects the flavor and tradition of its location.

Schooled in both fine arts and architecture, the Boston-born designer has always headed his own firm. For more than 25 years he has specialized exclusively in hotels; being responsible for most of the Ritz-Carlton Hotels—some 30 to date—and a great many of those of Four Seasons Ltd. He has also designed interiors for such beloved old landmarks as the Pierre in New York and the Olympic in Seattle, and for independent hotels from Sardinia to Bangkok. Current projects are in locations in Europe, the Far East, the Pacific Rim, as well as in the United States.

Mr. Nicholson's work has received many awards for excellence. In 1987, he received the restaurant and hotel design Platinum Circle Award for interior design. His work has also been featured in books and publications of the world's best hotels.

Classic pillars lead visitors down the central corridor of this residence.

In a spacious library, cases displaying the client's impressive book collection alternate with large windows for a serene, sunlit atmosphere.

An intimate cocktail salon.

Mrs. Henry Parish II

A sense of continuity is extremely important in the decoration of houses according to Mrs. Henry Parish II, or "Sister" Parish, as she is known to friends and colleagues. She likes the feeling of permanence, and a beauty that comes from living with family and treasures. She says that "without taste, all the knowledge in the world won't help you make a room look right." While talking of simple charm and comfort, Sister Parish's trained eye and natural instinct about design produces rooms that are vibrant and memorable.

After her marriage in 1930, the young couple's first house in New York was decorated by Mrs. Brown of McMillen. When they took a small house in New Jersey, Mrs. Parish did it up herself. Friends admired her flair and asked if she could do something with the rather time-worn living room of the Essex Hunt Club—thus a decorating career was launched.

In 1963, Sister Parish formed a partnership with Albert Hadley. Their firm, Parish-Hadley Associates, has completed design projects throughout the world, including private residences for Mrs. Vincent Astor, Mr. and Mrs. Gordon Getty, Mrs. John Hay Whitney, and Mr. and Mrs. Henryk de Kwiatkowski. Although opposed to radical change and so called "trends," the firm's work is frequently very innovative. Sister Parish has been quoted as saying: "Innovation is often the ability to reach into the past and bring back what is good, what is beautiful, what is useful, what is lasting."

The drawing room of Mrs. Henry Parish II features an artful combination of 18th Century English and French furnishings and licorice enamel walls (1960s).

Mrs. Enid Haupt's passion for flowers is reflected in her living room. 18th Century French furniture is arranged in classic French taste, Parc de Versailles (1985).

A sculpted ceiling by Arp canopies Mrs. Nelson Rockefeller's living room overlooking Central Park. Rug is hand-woven horsehair; Japanese screen is 17th Century.

Charles Pfister

With the philosophy he called "opulence without waste," Charles Pfister influenced corporate, residential and product design across the United States and overseas. His creations include the '21' Club in New York; Weyerhauser Headquarters in Tacoma; California First Bank in San Francisco; the Four Seasons Hotel in Milan; Shell Central in The Hague; the Grand Hotel in Washington, D.C.; the Deutschebank Headquarters in Frankfurt; and Knoll International in Paris, Brussels and New York.

Mr. Pfister earned his bachelor of architecture degree at the University of California and completed graduate work at the Rudolph Schaeffer School of Design. He spent 15 years with the San Francisco offices of Skidmore, Owings and Merrill, during which he rose to the head of the firm's interior design department. In 1981, with three people and a small office, he founded Charles Pfister Associates. Adding a London office in 1987, he renamed the firm The Pfister Partnership in 1988. It soon grew to a staff of 50 in London and San Francisco. Along with interior and furniture design, the company produced lighting, textile and carpet designs.

In 1986, *Interiors* magazine named Mr. Pfister designer of the year. The design community was saddened by Charles Pfister's death in 1990. In the 1990 Hall of Fame issue of *Interior Design* magazine, Stanley Abercrombie wrote that "Charles was an extraordinary designer, an extraordinary friend, an extraordinary man. He demanded quality for himself as well as for his clients, and he knew, better than anyone else what quality was."

Knoll International Paris Showroom spaces were opened up by cutting away the walls with a stepped profile. Light, trees and views of street activity are brought to the back of the narrow space with the use of mirrors.

Mr. Pfister designed all of the interiors, finishes and much of the furniture and lighting for the Royal Dutch/Shell Central Headquarters, The Hague. Pictured here is the board room with a custom table surrounded by Pfister designed chairs for Knoll International.

The "21" Club, New York City, was a favorite but challenging project. The goal was to refresh a landmark without upsetting loyal clientele. Lighting in particular was completely updated.

Warren Platner

Warren Platner, a Fellow member of the American Institute of Architects, earned his bachelor of architecture degree from Cornell University and worked for Eero Saarinen Associates for 15 years before opening his own office in New Haven in 1965. His style is marked by a penchant for sensuous materials—soft fabrics, leather, sculpted wool and silk walls; fine woods, marble and granite; glass, mirrors and highly polished metals that set up multiple reverberations to enliven spaces—carefully lit and controlled for a single aesthetic statement.

Among his most important projects are Kent Memorial Library in Suffield, Connecticut; Princeton University Prospect Center; Mortgage Guarantee Investment Corporation, Water Tower Place in Chicago; Windows on the World, World Trade Center in Manhattan; Providence Athenaeum; Sea Containers Headquarters in London; the ships *Fantasia* and *Fiesta* and Wildflower Restaurant Lodge in Vail, Colorado and several elegant private residences. His furniture designs for Knoll and his bathroom fixtures for American Standard are universally known and in use around the world. Mr. Platner has been the recipient of the Rome Prize in Architecture, a Fulbright advanced research award in architecture; a Graham Foundation award for advanced studies in the fine arts; and the Designers Lighting Forum first annual award. A President's Fellow of the Rhode Island School of Design, and a Fellow of the American Academy in Rome, Mr. Platner has lectured at several museums and universities.

The windows at the Sea Containers House in London, the headquarters for an international shipping, railroad and hotel company, provide an impressive vista of the river and the city.

Landscape and gardens designed by Mr. Platner create natural views and a feeling of privacy at the Friedman residence in Greenwich, Connecticut. The rooms of the Friedman residence echo the gardens outside using natural elements such as unadorned wood, stone and textiles, many handwoven by Mr. Platner.

In Columbus, Ohio at the Porter Wright Morris & Arthur Headquarters, conference rooms look onto a day-lit garden atrium.

The confined spaces at the Carlyle Hotel in New York focus on detailed walls and ceilings, decorative fabrics and the soft architectural quality of framing and paneling with fabric.

Donald D. Powell and Robert D. Kleinschmidt

Donald Powell and Robert Kleinschmidt began their partnership nearly 20 years ago with years of relevant experience behind them and dreams of producing the best classic modernist design in the country. Today, in their hometown Chicago and across the nation, they are renowned for their expertise in the field.

With academic training that included graduate study following their baccalaureate degrees, and more than a decade in the Chicago office of Skidmore, Owings and Merrill, they established the Powell/Kleinschmidt offices in 1976. Their practice is characterized by an incorporation of exterior architectural elements into the interior spaces, an effective translation of the client's programmatic needs into a coherent plan, and adherence to budgetary guidelines.

Their success can be judged by such award-winning projects as the Northwestern University School of Law, the Mayer, Brown & Platt law offices, Woodwork Corporation of America corporate offices and the LaSalle Partners corporate offices.

Both designers are active in cultural, civic, and educational activities in the Chicago community.

This 1,700 sq. ft. Lake Shore Drive apartment in Chicago, Illinois (1985) was created to echo the architecture of the building, which was designed by Mies van der Rohe.

An 18,000 sq. ft. project in a large Midwest banking and financial institution (1989) included this reception area for dining and the board room.

The 12,000 sq. ft. project at the executive offices of the Chicago Mercantile Exchange (1987) involved redesigning the entire floor. Pictured here is the view of the reception area to the executive offices.

A three-story greenhouse welcomes employees and clients to the main entrance via a bridge at the Merryville, Indiana offices of The Prudential Insurance Company of America (1978).

A biomorphic dining room banquette recalls the curved facade of the 1919 Mies van der Rohe building of a Lake Shore Drive apartment (1985). The space maximizes the view and light from Lake Michigan.

William Pulgram

Born in Vienna, Austria, William Pulgram received a bachelor of architecture degree from the Georgia Institute of Technology. He went on to study at the Ecole des Beaux Arts in Fontainebleau, France, where he was awarded first prize in architectural design.

Based on the philosophy that interior design is a continuation of the architecture of a space, Mr. Pulgram founded Associated Space Design, Inc. in Atlanta in 1963. The firm's work received much recognition under his leadership, especially for projects focusing on user-responsive interior environments for clients such as Southern Bell, Coca-Cola and Black & Decker. Extensive research into automation of the work place spurred Mr. Pulgram to co-author the book *Designing the Automated Office* (1984), which has been translated into Japanese and won the Designer's Book Club Book of the Month Award.

Now Chairman Emeritus of Associated Space Design, Mr. Pulgram consults nationally and internationally on architecture and facilities planning. He is a frequent speaker and panel member on man-made environments, with special emphasis on the information-based society. Mr. Pulgram's involvement in the profession includes membership in the National Committee on Interiors, Associated Institute of Architects (AIA); the Architectural Research Council, AIA Foundation; and the Atlanta Arts Association.

The Old Post Office in Washington D.C. (1979) was an adaptive restoration. It was the first such project of the U.S. government and part of the Pennsylvania Avenue Redevelopment Project.

At the Tampa Electric Company, Tampa, Florida (1979), adjacent offices overlook a spectacular atrium.

The ground floor arcade and art gallery at the Hurt Building Redevelopment (1985), Atlanta, Georgia.

Andrée Putman

"Andrée Putman is a designer with her roots in the thirties but her finger firmly on the pulse of contemporary design...her work brings together modern lines and materials with classic elements from the past."

Andrée Putman, a native of Paris, has influenced nearly every area of design with her style and grace. Before embarking on her current career, she studied piano at the Paris Conservatoire, worked as a journalist, was associated with the French store Prisunic and was a marketing consultant in the fashion community.

Ms. Putman's interiors span the globe and have gained her worldwide recognition. Just a few of her projects are: the fashion boutiques of Yves St. Laurent, Karl Lagerfeld, Thierry Mugler, Carita and Azzedine Alaïa; model apartments for Manhattan's Metropolitan Tower and U.N. Plaza buildings; the Morgan Hotel in New York; projects for Ebel; and the Musée d'Art Contemporain de Bordeaux. Ms. Putman's product designs include flatware, silver, crystal, tableware, textiles, carpets and rugs, towels, sheets and even mannequins.

In 1978, she founded the studios Ecart and Ecart International, located in Paris' 16th arrondissement. Due largely to Ecart, pieces by Eileen Gray, Mallet-Stevens, Fortuny, Gaudi, Herbst and Frank have been rescued from oblivion.

The massive Wasserturm Hotel in Cologne, erected between 1868-1872, is the largest water tower in Europe. Ms. Putman integrated new hotel functions into the challenging circular architecture while preserving its original character.

The "maisonette" suites at the Wasserturm are on two levels. Here, armchairs face a banquette with reading lights on each wing; a lit sand-blasted glass wall glows softly and hides the stairs leading to the bedroom.

Ms. Putman utilized the circular motif in even the smallest details to create a feeling of sensuality and echo the architecture throughout the Wasserturm, as seen in shot of a bathroom.

A black koolshade screen covers the exterior of the Hotel Le Lac in Kawaguchiko, Japan (near Toyko).

A sliding glass screen of translucent glass with flush mounted mirrors forms a backdrop for a double sink at the Hotel Le Lac. The sink bowl is preformed polished concrete; its stand is covered in glass mosaic tile.

Luminous columns and a side table covered in grès céramé tile accent the salon of a suite at the Hotel Le Lac. The suspended writing desk is painted in Nextel; armchairs are Ecart S.A.

Rita St. Clair

Rita St. Clair, president of the Baltimore based firm that bears her name, is noted for her work in hotels, restaurants, offices, condominiums, and above all, renovation and historic preservation—an interest which antedates the current preservation movement by many years. She traces it to her undergraduate years as a fine arts and art history major at the University of Iowa and to her long time residence in Baltimore, a city rich in historic structures.

Ms. St. Clair is a fellow member of the American Society of Interior Designers (ASID). As a speaker for the National Trust for Historic Preservation and an active participant in ASID's Speakers Network, she lectures frequently to students, professionals, and preservation groups.

Her major projects include the interior renovations for City Hall, Center Stage Theater, the Octagon House at the United States Fidelity and Guarantee campus, Peabody Court Hotel and other Baltimore landmarks; Palmer House Hotel in Chicago; the Netherland Plaza Hotel in Cincinnati; Le Pavillon and The Prime Rib restaurants in Washington, D.C.

Ms. St. Clair, who also studied at Parsons School of Design in New York and the Musée des Arts Decoratifs in Paris, is the recipient of a number of design awards for both products and interior projects from ASID, the American Institute of Architects, the Art Deco Societies of America, Illuminating Engineering Society, the Hardwood Institute, and others. In 1979, she served as national president of ASID.

A restoration of an 1870s room, including decorative architectural elements, at the Baltimore City Hall. While furnishings are new, many are reproductions of the original pieces.

Overleaf: Originally a great hall, this space was transformed into an elegant dining room, cocktail lounge and bar.

John F. Saladino

John F. Saladino, born in Kansas City, Missouri, is a graduate of Notre Dame and the Yale School of Art and Architecture.
His earliest career experience was in Rome with architect Piero Sartoga. In 1972, he returned to New York to open his own design practice which has grown into a full-service architectural and interior design organization. The practice's current projects include residential interiors, residential architecture, restorations and large office headquarters. Well known for his scholarly interest in the work of the great Italian Renaissance architect Andrio Palladio, Mr. Saladino combines historical references with simple, modern forms. "From the Villa of Mysteries in Pompeii through Palladio and William Kent, there is a genuine love of history that permeates all of Saladino's designs," reports his staff. He has one foot in the headquarters of ancient design, the other firmly planted in the present day.
Mr. Saladino has successfully extended his design practice into the field of furniture design with collections for Baker, Knapp & Tubbs, Bloomingdale's, Dunbar, and David Edwards. In 1986, he launched his own furniture company with 60 of his designs.
Mr. Saladino's work is published regularly in the United States, England, France, Germany, Italy and Japan. He is a board member for a number of organizations including Formica, Parsons School of Design and Steuben Glass. Numerous awards include four Daphne Awards for furniture design.

A signature Saladino surface since 1970, scratch-coat plaster walls envelope a mixture of modern and antique furnishings.

Eight foot high folding screens of antique wallpaper and high-backed sofas humanize the monumental scale of this room.

Betty S. Sherrill

Betty Stevens Sherrill is respected in many circles, not only for her distinguished career in interior design, but also for her active involvement in numerous civic, cultural and philanthropic activities.

A New Orleans native, Mrs. Sherrill attended Newcomb College. In 1949, she married Virgil Sherrill and began study at Parsons School of Design. She went to McMillen in 1951 and became Assistant to the President, Eleanor Brown. In 1975, she was appointed president and chief executive officer of the firm, a post she holds today.

Mrs. Sherrill has served as vice president of the Boys Club of New York and as officer and member of the Board of Directors of the National Trust of New York State, as well as a member of the board of Southampton Hospital and Sloan Kettering Memorial Hospital.

Interested in the development of professional education in interior design, Mrs. Sherrill has been working on a project to fund a joint program at Tulane University between the School of Architecture and the art department. She received an honorary doctorate degree as Outstanding Alumna of the Year in 1987 from Tulane. She is also a member of the Board of Trustees of Loyola University. Mrs. Sherrill has lectured extensively across the country.

Betty S. Sherrill

Marble floors and a magnificent Regency console with a Louis XVI mirror and Kandler bird candelabra form a grand welcome in a New York City maisonette entrance hall.

Another view of the same entry shows a Rodin sculpture atop a skirted table. Gracie wallpaper. Louis XVI bergère.

With yellow moiré painted walls, Aubusson rug, and 18th century chandeliers and candles as the principal light, this New York drawing room exudes a warm glow.

Sally Sirkin Lewis

The harmonic mesh of opposites animates the work of Sally Sirkin Lewis—modern art mixes with antiquities, and classical architectural elements amplify contemporary motifs.

In the mid 1950s, Mrs. Lewis began her career as an apprentice in various East Coast architecture and design firms, handling all phases of residential, corporate, contract and hospitality projects.

Subsequently, she opened her own firm in New York City and Miami before moving to Los Angeles. After working as a project designer for a large contract and hospitality design company, she opened her present firm, Sally Sirkin Interior Design, in 1969.

She designs interiors for hotels, corporate offices, yachts, showrooms, residences and private aircraft. She is also president of J. Robert Scott & Associates, Incorporated, which features her own furniture and textile designs, and represents leading national manufacturers of home furnishings. J. Robert Scott has showrooms in Los Angeles, Laguna Niguel and New York City.

Sally Sirkin Interior Design projects include designs for Warnaco, Incorporated in New York and Los Angeles; Mr. and Mrs. Takami Takahashi in Japan, Thailand and Los Angeles; Dr. and Mrs. Kihong Kwon in Los Angeles; and singer Joni Mitchell in Bel-Air and Malibu, California.

Mrs. Lewis is a frequent guest lecturer at university design classes and for numerous association conventions.

An ambience of understatement yet classical strength emanates from the J. Robert Scott New York showroom. Furniture is designed by Ms. Lewis; custom panels by Evans & Brown.

In a Los Angeles family's formal dining room, a contemporary art collection curated by Ms. Lewis complements monolithic contemporary furniture.

Along with designing the interiors for this project in Japan, Ms. Lewis curated a collection of contemporary art for her clients. A Morris Louis "Veil" provides a serene background.

Black leather upholstery and neutral backgrounds are an ideal setting for the art and artifacts in the home of Sally Sirkin Lewis and her husband.

Minimal furnishings accompany elegant architecture and artwork in the classic formal living room of the Los Angeles family.

Ethel Smith

The vitality and brilliance of Ethel Smith have inspired those around her throughout her extraordinary career.

After attending boarding school in Englewood, New Jersey, Mrs. Smith went to New York School of Fine and Applied Arts, now Parsons School of Design. She spent two years studying in New York and a third in Europe. Her first job was with R.H. Macy, where she claims the "practical training was invaluable." In 1929, Mrs. Smith came to McMillen and worked under Eleanor Brown. Since she was the youngest member of the firm, Mrs. Smith was allowed to carry the samples for Eleanor Brown, "which was a privilege."

In her early years as an assistant, Mrs. Smith worked for the Honorable Myron Taylor, Doris Duke, the Countess Szechenyi, Marshall Field, and the James McDonnells, among others. Her reputation for impeccable taste and style brought her innumerable clients later as well: the Honorable Winthrop Aldrich, the Honorable Douglas Dillon, the Edward Bembergs, Josephine Abercrombie, the private apartments at the White House during the Johnson administration, and much of Blair House. She has worked on clubs and offices as well as private residences.

Mrs. Smith still lives in the neighborhood of New York City where she was born in 1905, "in the shadow of the Queensboro Bridge." After 60 years of work, she still says that, "Each new job is a challenge and each new one is my favorite. Large or small, I enjoy them all."

A rug from Patterson Flynn is the perfect accent for exquisite American antiques in the entry of this Southampton home designed by Stanford White.

Regency chairs encircle an English 19th Century table in the dining room of the same home.

A pair of 18th Century English armchairs and a Venetian 19th Century mirror in a gracious mahogany paneled New York City living room.

In the same room, 18th Century English tables and chairs with V'soske rug, English chintz and 19th Century French flower paintings form an inviting arrangement.

Curtains and furniture in red velvet and a contemporary red and white rug create a rich ambiance in a card room in New York City. Chairs are reproduction Smith and Watson.

A leopard rug, green moire walls and contemporary bronze table and mirror combine in the entry to a home in New York City; over-doors were constructed for architectural detail.

Andre Staffelbach

Andre Staffelbach, a former national president of the Institute of Business Designers, was born in Chur, Switzerland. Having completed his apprenticeship in interior design and studies at the Kunstgewerbeschule Luzern and Zurich, he worked with leading design firms in his native country.
Mr. Staffelbach came to the United States in 1962. In 1966, he founded the firm bearing his name in Dallas. The firm merged with Interior Spaces of Kansas City, Missouri, and Topeka, Kansas in 1985 and became Staffelbach Designs and Associates.
In following the philosophy that, "Through the thoughtful exploration and integration of form, space, materials and resources, we achieve interior spaces of quality and significance which express our overall commitment to excellence from concept through realization," Mr. Staffelbach has built an impressive client roster—Apple Computer, American Airlines, Equitable Life, Frito-Lay, GTE, Holiday Inns, IBM, Mobil Oil Corporation, Prudential-Bache and Rosewood Properties are just a sampling of the list.
The firm's staff has grown to include over 50 designers, architects and support personnel. Mr. Staffelbach has been honored with awards from numerous professional organizations and has lectured at seminars and symposia across the country.

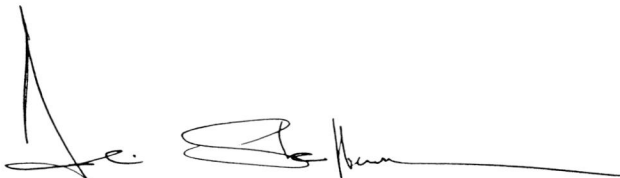

The corporate entry and building reception of Bozell, Inc., Irving, Texas. Glass, granite, stainless steel and black leather support a forward-thinking global business climate.

Redesign of the executive offices at Bozell, Inc. blends classic elements of the past with state-of-the-art furnishings.

Antiques harmonize with the high-tech interior of the President's office at Bozell, Inc. A glass block filters natural light into all interior spaces of the offices.

Philippe Starck

Function seasoned with ingenious wit distinguishes Philippe Starck's manifold creations. His imagination attends a sweeping range of furniture, hotels, company buildings and office blocks, luggage, pasta, lighting, residences (including a suite of rooms in the Elysée Palace commissioned by French President Mitterand in 1983), hardware, a bridge, cutlery and a melange of other objects and spaces.

A design school dropout, Mr. Starck's training was unconventional and largely self-taught. As a small boy, he sat beneath his aircraft designer father's desk, a sketch pad and pencil in hand, and redesigned his toys.

At 17, a passion to design racing car seats foreshadowed his multiple chair designs, which are particularly prized by design enthusiasts. "All my product is first, first, first function... my work has nothing to do with culture...with the aesthetic...I work directly with the field of evidence."

In the 1970s, his creation of two popular nightclubs in Paris, La Main Bleue and Les Bains Douches, secured his eminence in the world of interior design. Other projects followed: Teatrix Restaurant in Madrid; The Royalton in New York; and the Osahi in Japan. In addition to receiving awards for work in the United States, Europe and Japan, many of Mr. Starck's designs are housed in the permanent collections of American and European museums.

A unique vase by Daum in the lobby of the Royalton Hotel in New York.

The lobby leads guests into the Royalton Hotel.

The grand entrance to the Royalton Hotel.

A contemporary and inviting vignette in a bedroom.

The glistening sink in the adjoining bathroom.

The contrasts of dark and light are joined by the circular motif in the "Bar des Conspiratores."

The classical lines of this bed look sleek but comfortable.

Stanley Tigerman and Margaret McCurry

Stanley Tigerman and Margaret McCurry have led distinguished careers both separately and together since 1982. A native Chicagoan, Mr. Tigerman received architectural degrees from Yale. He worked with Skidmore, Owings and Merrill's Chicago offices, and Paul Rudolph and Harry Weese before opening his own office in 1962. He has written many books on architecture and is the Director of the School of Architecture at the University of Illinois at Chicago.

Ms. McCurry, who earned her degree at Vassar and a Loeb fellowship at Harvard's Graduate School of Design, opened her own office in 1977, and lectures widely.

In the past decade the two architects have collaborated on many of the firm's projects, including their own Architects' Weekend House in Michigan, the Knoll International Park and Showroom in Houston, and showrooms for Formica and Thonet. Other notable projects include the Energy Museum for Commonwealth Edison; housing in Fukuoka, Japan and Berlin, Germany; the installation exhibit for the Art Institute of Chicago's "Chicago Architecture: 1872-1922," the Study Center at the Art Institute; decorative objects for Swid-Powell, and a sterling silver tea service for Alessi.

Individually and together, the principals have received awards for distinguished architecture from the American Institute of Architects (AIA), *Architectural Record*, *Progressive Architecture*, Yale University, and Pratt Institute. Mr. Tigerman and Ms. McCurry are both fellows of the American Institute of Architects (AIA).

In this North Shore residence in Chicago, Illinois (1991), each space rotates off of another. A meandering "street" with functions organized as a village replaces the conventional notion of a foyer.

Overleaf: Combining Gothic verticality with gestures to Mies van der Rohe and Eliel Saarinen, the offices of the Chicago Bar Association (1990) reflect the hallowed stature of the 115-year-old institution.

Adam D. Tihany

Fluent in Hungarian, Hebrew, Italian and English, Adam D. Tihany was born in Transylvania on New Year's Day. Raised in Jerusalem, he was schooled in Milan, where he graduated from the Politecnico di Milano, School of Architecture and Urban Planning. In 1978, he brought his talent to New York City and established Adam D. Tihany International, Ltd. Following the Italian philosophy of involvement in the total design process, the firm offers everything from product design to commercial and residential interiors.

Often called a chameleon for his ability to realize the essence of his client's personality in his work, Adam Tihany once said in an interview "...the client does not have to have a clear idea of what he wants to do. All he has to have is personality—an outlook on life, a point of view, an aspiration."

While the majority of his work is commercial, Mr. Tihany will take on an occasional residential project. He is most famous for his restaurant designs, which number over 100 here and abroad. Among those are Bice Restaurants in Miami, Atlanta, Scottsdale, San Diego, Madrid, Paris and Mexico City; Biba in Boston; Berlin's Hard Rock Cafe; Gundel in Budapest; Trader Vic's worldwide; and La Coupole, Metro, Huberts, Malvasia and Le Cirque in New York. In 1987, with chef Francesco Antonucci, Mr. Tihany opened the Venetian style Remi in New York, and later, in Santa Monica. He has also completed a myriad of hotel installations including the Doubletree Inn in Santa Clara, California and the Drake Swissotel in New York, along with shop and showroom designs on both coasts. Products he has designed range from a furniture line for Pace to vodka and martini glasses for Absolut.

A view of the bar and dining area from the entranceway at Remi New York.

The restaurant Biba in Boston.

In the dining area at Remi New York, handpainted murals by Paulin Paris create European atmosphere.

The dining area at Bice in Los Angeles.

Looking down on the bar at Bice in Los Angeles.

Carleton Varney

Carleton Varney is renowned for the decoration and restoration of hotels and resorts in the Caribbean, Europe and the United States, and for the use of unexpected vibrant colors which kindle his designs.

Mr. Varney also enjoys an esteemed reputation as a writer. His syndicated newspaper column, *Your Family Decorator*, appears three times a week in scores of newspapers across the country. The author of 20 books, most offering practical decorating advice for the layman, he has also written an autobiography and a biography of Dorothy Draper, the design trendsetter who established Dorothy Draper and Company, the firm Mr. Varney has headed since 1965.

From his offices in New York, West Virginia, London and St. Croix in the U.S. Virgin Islands, he directs his firm's projects, which recently included the official residence of the vice president of the United States. His "panache and flair" have led to a full lecture schedule, and to his selection as design consultant for many functions at the White House.

In 1983, Mr. Varney founded the Carleton Varney School of Art and Design at the University of Charleston in West Virginia.

This suite at the Waldorf Towers was designed with the legendary clientele of the hotel in mind.

Overleaf: Rich fabrics and deep "royal" colors enhance the grandeur of the main gallery at the Dromland Castle in Ireland.

The Vignelli Associates offices in New York City.

Lella and Massimo Vignelli

Lella and Massimo Vignelli are internationally celebrated for the refined, classic aesthetics of their graphics, interiors and products. Working from New York offices since the 1960s, they have dominated the modern graphics of a generation and are true touchstones of our age.

"Whenever Lella and Massimo Vignelli tackle a project, they are impelled by a desire for essence. The Vignellis love taut thinking. They never add anything when creating; rather, they remove, they subtract," writes a biographer in one important volume published by Rizzoli about this pair of design giants.

The Vignellis have nurtured numerous fine designers in their firm who have gone on to found important design practices.

They continue to mentor emerging talents. Appropriate to their role as leaders in the world community of designers, the Vignellis often achieve the essence of the Renaissance concept called "sprezzatura", which roughly means they achieve excellence with effortless grace. Many of the firm's works have been cited as masterpieces of contemporary design and are included in the collection of The Museum of Modern Art, as well as other museum collections.

The number and type of international awards they have received in several fields attests to their ability to transfer the essence of their intellectual design process to several fields. As 1988 recipients of the Hall of Fame honor, it is appropriate that they have directed the graphic development of this book.

The Poltrona Frau Showroom, Milan.

In Modena, Italy, the Poltrona Frau Showroom.

Kenneth H. Walker

Painter, graphic artist, interior designer, product designer and architect, Ken Walker is professionally active in all aspects of design. He graduated from Brown University and received a masters in architecture from the Harvard University Graduate School of Design. In 1970, Ken Walker founded the Walker Group of which he is president and CEO. With the 1985 acquisition of a retail planning firm (Copeland, Novak and Israel), the name was changed to WalkerGroup/CNI. Today, the firm is active in product development and is at the forefront of computer aided design. The staff of more than 100 architects, retail and corporate designers, graphic and industrial designers work on projects worldwide.
Mr. Walker is a member of the American Institute of Architects (AIA); the Young Presidents' Organization; the Institute of Store Planners; the Society of Architectural Historians; and the Architecture and Design Committee of the Museum of Modern Art in New York. He has taught at Rhode Island School of Design, Harvard University, the Massachusetts Institute of Technology and the Architectural Association in London.
A member of the AIA Drawing Committee and a former member of the Historic Buildings Committee of the AIA, Mr. Walker is committed to historical preservation and adaption.

The Galleria store for Burdine's, Fort Lauderdale, Florida (1980), was designed as a flexible shell. A steel matrix atrium serves as a merchandising display and information source.

Galeries Lafayette features custom designed fixtures, brushed steel floors, free floating walls and cantilevered visual displays.

The renovation and expansion of the Saks Fifth Avenue flagship store; pictured is the men's department.

Another view of the men's department in New Tower of Saks Fifth Avenue.

Galeries Lafayette in New York City is a French retailer's first entry into the United States. A modern yet classic design is used.

Tod Williams and Billie Tsien

Partners in their firm since 1987, Tod Williams and Billie Tsien have produced a body of work small in quantity but large in felt presence—interiors for Asia Society, a downtown branch for the Whitney Museum, a conference room for *Vogue* magazine; an installation at the Walker Art Center in Minneapolis for the "Architecture Tomorrow" series; dormitories at Princeton and the University of Virginia and apartments and lofts in Manhattan.

Mr. Williams earned bachelor of arts and master of fine arts degrees from Princeton and worked for Richard Meier before receiving the Rome Prize in 1983. Ms. Tsien, who holds fine arts and architecture degrees from Yale and the University of California, Los Angeles, participated as an artist in the "Art on the Beach" series of collaborative installations at Battery Park City in Manhattan early in her career.

Working as a husband and wife team, Mr. Williams explores the physical and philosophical nature of construction while Ms. Tsien approaches design from a fine arts stance. Together, they have received design awards from the American Institute of Architects, *Architecture* magazine, *Progressive Architecture, Architectural Record,* and a grant from the New York State Council of the Arts.

A sliding glass panel, aluminum column and gold leaf wall are a unique combination in the Vogue magazine conference room, New York City.

The "Domestic Arrangement" installation at the Walker Art Museum. *The Spiegel pool house, Kings Point, New York.*

HALL OF FAME MEMBER ROSTER

1985
Davis Allen
Benjamin Baldwin
Florence Knoll Bassett
Mario Buatta
Barbara D'Arcy
Angelo Donghia
Henry End
Arthur Gensler
Richard Himmel
Melanie Kahane
Lawrence Lerner
Mrs. Henry Parish II
Warren Platner
John F. Saladino
Michael Taylor
Kenneth Walker

Special Award Recipient
Paige Rense,
Editor-in-Chief of
Architectural Digest.

1986
Marvin B. Affrime
Ward Bennett
Joseph Braswell
Joseph P. D'Urso
Albert Hadley
Mark Hampton
Howard Hirsch
Sarah Tomerlin Lee
Charles Pfister
Jay Spectre
Sally Walsh

Special Award Recipients
Benjamin D. Holloway,
Former Vice-Chairman of the
Equitable Real Estate Group,
Inc.; major art patron.

Diantha Nype,
Director of Public Relations for
Kips Bay Decorator Showhouse.

1987
Steve Chase
Jack Dunbar
Margo Grant
Bruce Gregga
Anthony Hail
William Hodgins
Neville Lewis
William Pulgram
Andrée Putman
Ethel Smith

Special Award Recipients
Robert O. Anderson,
Chairman and CEO of Hondo
Oil; former Chairman and
CEO of ARCO; pioneer in
underwriting the work of
professional designers.

Jeremiah Goodman,
interior designer and
illustrator of *Interior Design
Magazine*'s covers through
the 1960s.

1988
Kaleef Alaton
Orlando Diaz-Azcuy
Billy W. Francis
Charles Gwathmey
David Hicks
Edith Hills
Juan Montoya
Frank Nicholson
Andre Staffelbach
Robert Siegel
Lella Vignelli
Massimo Vignelli

Special Award Recipients
Stanley Barrows,
Parsons School of Design
faculty member, 1946-68;
former Chairman and faculty
member of the Fashion
Institute of Technology.

Olga Gueft
Editor of *Interiors*, 1945-80;
journalist, critic, photographer.

1989
Richard Carlson
Robert Currie
Jacques Grange
Mel Hamilton
Robert D. Kleinschmidt
Sally Sirkin Lewis
Donald D. Powell
Rita St. Clair
Betty Sherrill

Special Award Recipients
Jaime Ardiles-Arce,
renowned photographer
of interiors.

Sherman R. Emery,
Editor of *Interior Design
Magazine*, 1960-83.

1990
Louis M.S. Beal
Maria Bergson
Robert Bray
Thomas Britt
Frank Gehry
Margaret McCurry
Michael Schaible
Philippe Starck
Stanley Tigerman
Billie Tsien
Carleton Varney
Tod Williams

Special Award Recipients
Lester Dundes,
Vice President and Publishing
Director of *Interior Design.*

Ruth K. Lynford,
interior designer and lobbyist
who headed the campaign for
interior design certification in
the state of New York; former
National Chairman of
Education for the American
Society of Interior Designers.

Ian Schrager,
prominent patron of
architecture; owner of the
Paramount, Royalton and
Morgans hotels; the force
behind the legendary
nightclubs Studio 54 and the
Palladium.

1991
Scott Bromley
Don Brinkmann
Michael Graves
Naomi Leff
Robert Metzger
Adam Tihany

Special Award Recipients
Philip E. Kelley,
Chairman Emeritus of the
Merchandise Mart in Chicago;
former head of Baker Knapp &
Tubbs Furniture.

Santo Loquasto,
Set designer for Woody Allen's
movies and other prestigious
theater productions.

The Henry Francis du Pont
Winterthur Museum,
a museum of more than
89,000 objects from the 13
colonies begun by Francis du
Pont; Thomas Graves, Jr.,
Museum Director.

BIBLIOGRAPHY

Page 98
Abercrombie, S., *Gwathmey Siegel*, Whitney Library of Design, New York, NY, 1981.

Arnell, P. and Bickford, T., Ed., *Charles Gwathmey and Robert Siegel: Buildings and Projects, 1964-1984*, Harper & Row, New York, NY, 1984.

Page 22
Baldwin, B., *Billy Baldwin Decorates*, Holt, Rinehart & Winston, Orlando, FL, 1973.

Pages 190, 198
Brown, E., *Sixty Years of Interior Design: The World of McMillen*, Viking Press, New York, NY, 1982.

Page 220
Caribbean Travel and Life, May/June, 1992.

Page 224
Celant, G., Constantine, M., McFadden, D., and Rykwert, J., *Design: Vignelli*, Rizzoli International Publications, New York, NY, 1990.

Page 182
Christian Science Monitor, March 27, 1992.

Editor & Publisher, January 25, 1986

Page 232
Gandee, Charles K., "Exploring Space", *HG*, October, 1991

Page 106
Greene, E., *Mark Hampton on Decorating*, Conde Naste Books, Division of Random House, New York, NY, 1989.

Haute Decor, February, 1991.

Page 112
Hicks, D., *On Living With Taste*, McMillen, New York, NY, 1969.

House Beautiful, October, 1991.

Page 56
Interior Design, December, 1987.

Page 68
Interior Design, 1988

Page 82, 116
Interior Design, 1985

Page 220
Interior Design, December, 1990; February, 1986; March, 1990; May, 1990.

Interiors, July, 1985; November, 1985.

Page 220
The Irish Times, Dublin, Ireland, September 16, 1988.

Pages 56, 194
Rense, P., *The AD 100*, Architectural Digest Publishing Corporation, New York, NY, 1990.

Rense, P., *Designers' Own Homes*, The Knapp Press, Los Angeles, CA, 1984.

Page 120
Restaurant Hotel Design International, November 1991

Page 178
Rousseau, F., *Andrée Putman: A Designer Apart*, Rizzoli International Publications, New York, NY, 1990.

Page 18
Slavin, Maeve, *Davis Allen: 40 Years of Interior Design at Skidmore, Owings and Merrill*, Rizzoli International Publications, New York, NY, 1990.

Page 116
Stoller, Ezra (foreword), *Ten By Warren Platner*, McGraw-Hill, New York, NY, 1975

Page 206
The Sunday Times Magazine, November 11, 1990

Page 212
Stanley Tigerman: Buildings & Projects, Rizzoli International Publications, New York, NY, 1989.

Page 182
Wall Street Journal, January 15, 1982.

PHOTOGRAPHY CREDITS

Peter Aaron, Esto
84-85, 231 (upper)

Gil Amiaga
229

Jaime Ardiles-Arce
19, 20, 21, 26, 30, 33, 39, 45 (all), 46 (all), 47 (upper left, lower left, lower right), 87, 88, 89, 121, 122-123, 124-125, 137, 147, 149, 161, 163, 164, 165, 169 (lower), 195, 196, 197 (all), 222-223

Morley Baer
83, 132 (all), 133 (left)

Adam Bartos
95, 96-97

Jonathan Becker
199 (all), 200 (all), 201 (all)

Antoine Bootz
127, 128, 129

Steven Brooks
92 (upper)

Dan Cornish, Esto
61, 62

George Cserna
183

Damora
131, 133 (right)

Phillip Ennis
79

Dan Forer
118-119

Tina Freeman
169 (upper)

A. Garrison, David Hewitt
92 (lower)

Jeff Goldberg, Esto
93

Francois Halard
34-35, 139, 140

Mick Hales (for *HG*)
23 (all)

Steve Hall, Hedrich-Blessing
214-215

Jim Hedrich, Hedrich-Blessing
173 (upper)

Hedrich-Blessing Photography
143

Lizzy Himmel
186-187

Wolfgang Hoyt
55 (all)

Elliot Kaufman
100-101

Dennis Krukowski
104-105, 148

Nathaniel Lieberman
136

Norman McGrath
29, 31, 184-185

Nick Merrick, Hedrich-Blessing
25, 27 (lower), 37, 38

Jon Miller, Hedrich-Blessing
171, 172 (all), 173 (lower), 203, 204, 205

Michael Moran
230 (all), 231 (lower), 233, 234, 235

Antonio Mulas
226

Melina Mulas
227

Kim Nichols
57, 58-59

Mary E. Nichols
80, 81, 196

Peter Paige
135, 141, 144-145, 217, 218 (all)

Paschall/Taylor
91

Warren Platner
167, 168 (all)

Karen Radkai
160

Mark Ross
15, 16, 17

John Spragg
113

Willam P. Steele
103

Brian Vanden Brink
63 (all)

Van Iknwegen Photography
213

Luca Vignelli
225

Peter Vitale
47 (upper right), 188-189, 191, 192, 193, 221

Deide Von Schaewen
179, 180 (all), 181

Paul Warchol
53, 54, 99

Nick Wheeler
27 (upper)

James Yochum
117

Toshi Yoshimi
69, 70, 71 (all), 219 (all)